Understanding the Human Mind

The Logical Thinking Process

Jason Browne

Table of Contents

INTRODUCTION 1

    ABOUT THE AUTHOR 6

CHAPTER 1: THE LOGICAL BRAIN 9

    LOGICAL THINKING 9

        Inductive Reasoning 10

        Deductive Reasoning 11

    TRADITIONAL BRAIN FUNCTION THEORIES 14

    NEUROSCIENTIFIC EVIDENCE 15

    BRAIN FUNCTIONS 18

        Neuroimagery 18

        Heterogenous Cerebral Network 20

CHAPTER 2: THE PRINCIPLES OF LOGIC 23

    THREE LAWS OF LOGIC 23

        The Law of Noncontradiction 24

        The Law of Excluded Middle 25

        The Principle of Identity 26

    THE FUNDAMENTALS OF THE LOGICAL/CRITICAL THINKING PROCESS ... 26

        The Nine Rules of Thinking Critically 27

        Critical Thinking Abilities 34

        Reason Logically 38

        Developing Arguments 40

    GOOD AND BAD ARGUMENTS 41

CHAPTER 3: IS YOUR BRAIN HOLDING YOU BACK? 45

    COGNITIVE BIAS 45

        Confirmation Bias 46

        Hindsight Bias 47

        Anchoring Bias 49

        The Misinformation Effect 50

The Actor Observer Bias *52*
The False Consensus Effect *53*
The Halo Effect *54*
The Self-Serving Bias *56*
The Availability Heuristic *57*
The Optimism Bias *62*
EMOTIONS 62
CRITICAL THINKING DISPOSITION 65

CHAPTER 4: WHY WE THINK ILLOGICALLY 68

CYNICISM 68
SKEPTICISM 71
NARROW-MINDEDNESS 73
RATIONALIZATION AND DOUBLETHINK 76
STRESS 77

**CHAPTER 5: 9 ACTIONABLE STRATEGIES FOR STRENGTHENING
LOGICAL THOUGHT 79**

1.   PRACTICE QUESTIONING 80
     Bloom's Taxonomy for Critical Thinking *80*
     How Questions are Used *83*
2.   BECOME AWARE OF YOUR MENTAL PROCESS 84
3.   SOCIALIZING 86
4.   DO LOGICAL THINKING EXERCISES 87
5.   PARTICIPATE IN DEBATES 92
6.   LEARN A NEW SKILL 93
7.   THINK IN REVERSE 94
8.   DO NOT ASSUME YOU ARE RIGHT 95
9.   WORK ON YOUR FOCUS AND CONCENTRATION 96

**CHAPTER 6: EXERCISING LOGICAL THOUGHT IN EVERYDAY LIFE
.... 100**

QUESTIONS AND SOCIAL MEDIA 100
LOGICAL DEBATES WITH FRIENDS 104
MAKE LOGICAL PURCHASE DECISIONS 106
STRENGTHEN COMMUNICATION 107
DISTANCE YOURSELF FROM FEELINGS 108
APPLY, APPLY, APPLY 112

CHAPTER 7: LANGUAGE, THOUGHT, AND LOGIC 114

LANGUAGE AND MATHEMATICS 115
AREAS RESPONSIBLE FOR LOGICAL THOUGHT..............................116
Word Choice 117
Vocabulary Definitions and Ambiguity 119
Interpretation 120
HOW TO BE A BETTER LOGICAL THINKER......................................121
Read More 121
Enrich Language 123
Soft Skills..123
Articulation 125
BECOMING A CRITICAL THINKER 125

CONCLUSION.. 127

REFERENCES.. 134

Introduction

"Excellence is never an accident. It is always the result of high intention, sincere effort, and intelligent execution; it represents the wise choice of many alternatives--choice, not chance, determines your destiny."

- Aristotle

For a long time, scientists believed that the brain was insignificant. In fact, ancient Egyptians thought so little of the organ that they would scoop it out, bit by bit, during the process of mummification. Later on, Aristotle believed that it was the location for the floating soul and that the heart was the main attraction to the human reasoning system. It was not until people started to notice that damage to the head caused abnormal behavior that many started to think that the brain was more important than initially believed.

Understanding the Human Mind: The Logical Thinking Process examines what it means to think logically. The brain's connections are infinitely complex, but breaking down the basics of understanding may make your life easier. Comprehending the functionality of the brain that makes learning easier and allows you to develop thought quicker. This book is the basis for basic human mind understanding.

Logical thinking is not an innate gift. Sure, humans have the ability to reason and string together logical thought, but it takes practice to master this skill. Reading signs both given by the environment and from your own experience is the basis for logical thinking. Logic is developed through playing games with our minds, giving the brain something on which to focus. Utilizing both logic and creativity make you better able to understand puzzles from mathematics to art.

Many believe that logical thinking is merely understanding the workings of the environment, something that animals cannot replicate. However, logical thought requires taking your opinions out of a situation and reasoning. For example, just because you may not like the taste of strawberries does not mean that they are poisonous. As a logical human, you are able to differentiate the difference between taste and inedibility.

Logical thought is also highly dependent on strategic thinking. Consider the business venture of starting a cupcake shop. You must contemplate the money required to rent or buy a space for your shop. Next, consider how many cupcakes you will need to make each day. This answer is different for new shops versus setting up a new location. You must also consider how much time you need to spend making the cupcakes. If you plan on making over 10,000 cupcakes daily, you may need to hire someone else to help out.

This oversimplified example gets to the point of understanding logic. A logical mind does not make decisions on a whim. It takes careful planning and understanding of not only your environment but your experiences to truly understand how to make your cupcake shop a success.

Logic requires an understanding of human language, both verbal and nonverbal. Interpreting words is the basis for logical thought. For example, if someone tells you that a meeting is mandatory, you are expected to fulfill the obligation. However, if someone tells you that a meeting is helpful, you may not feel bound to attend.

Even small, nonverbal cues determine your ability to reason. One of the most common examples of this is when people deny wanting something that they really desire. Logical people can pick up on these cues and form logical thought, ultimately understanding the true meaning of the words.

Critical thinking is severely lacking in today's society. Studies have shown that a massive 95% of grade schools do not add critical thinking to their curriculums, which means that a mass majority of the people leave high school without knowing how to think logically (Bouygues, 2018). Schools are not preparing people for the difficulties of life by making them participate in basic reasoning exercises.

However, this skill is far more important in life than simply being gifted. We have all heard a story about the kid in class who understood the subject matter better than anyone else, but he or she failed to transfer those skills to real-life situations. Ultimately, critical thinking is much more important than raw intelligence.

Critical thinking exercises are becoming more and more difficult to find, and social media and the internet play a large part in this. Today, people have access to a nearly unlimited supply of information. It is often forced on them through bombardments in Google searches or through social media.

Consider the last time you saw something you believed on social media. If you are like many people, it is likely that you believed what you saw. After all, why would people lie to you on social media? One of the leading examples of misinformation explained that people eat an average of eight spiders in their sleep every night. This information spread like wildfire, and soon people were claiming it as fact. However, the 'information' about spiders does not follow reason. Why would spiders go into your mouth when they tend their webs? Why would human mouths provide good hiding places for spiders? The study actually investigated how long it would take for false information to spread on the internet. If you have been duped by this false study, you are not the only one.

Misinformation like this flows freely through the internet. The more information is readily available to people, the easier it is to believe it is true. Many people have not thought critically for some time because others do the thinking for them. It is easier to believe that you are adversely affected by society than it is to believe that you may be the one who needs to change.

Schools today do not focus on the success of the student, rather on the information teachers can cram into pupils' minds to pass a test. Students are often silenced by teachers who do not want to hear contrary opinions. Classrooms are set up with a mixture of students instead of letting those who excel take more advanced classes, frustrating both students and parents.

Many college professors find it difficult to teach students because, though they are eager to learn, they have been cowed into believing that they must be fed answers. For many, it is more important to know the answers on a test than it is to understand the material. Unfortunately, many professors perpetuate these misguided practices, often making learning that much harder.

Fortunately, there are many tools that can help you gain those critical thinking skills that have been difficult to obtain in the past. This book, for example, teaches you how to think logically and critically. Through consistent practice, you will achieve the skills necessary to think critically.

Understanding the Human Mind: The Logical Thinking Process allows you to form your own opinions rationally. Many people today will avoid confrontation because they prefer to be in the right. However, thinking critically means that you will be able to debate with logical information and form your thoughts cohesively. You will be able to debate with yourself and others to develop your own thought style instead of using language from another source.

If you study this book closely, you will be able to develop a relationship with your mind and think clearly. You do not have to be stuck in a never-ending cycle of regurgitating information from others. Through this book, you will take control of your thoughts and opinions forever.

About the Author

Why do we do the things that we do? Are we often acting on impulse or is a certain force propelling us to act? These are just some of the questions that Jason Browne pondered in his teens and early adulthood.

Fascinated by the power of the human mind, Jason obtained his undergraduate psychology degree from Stony Brook University. Later on, he returned to his alma mater and completed a graduate program and a doctorate program in clinical psychology.

In his work with clients, Jason has been focusing on the empowerment of others and showing them how they can regain control of their existence, their confidence and even their mental processes. Through the years, he developed his unique therapeutic methodology focused on the power of the subconscious mind and the strategies for reprogramming it.

Understanding the Human Mind is Jason's series of books taking a look at numerous mental processes and how these could be strengthened. His work has also been presented in an array of reputable psychology journals.

Jason Browne lives and works in New York. He shares a beautiful cozy apartment with his partners and the most patient Siamese cat you've ever heard of.

Chapter 1:

The Logical Brain

Logical thinking is one of the most basic of human functions. It is what differentiates humans from animals. The ability to think for oneself is remarkable but is often overlooked because of its simplicity. For example, when was the last time you thought about the way you solve a problem? Much more occurs than pointing to one choice and hoping for success. Even if the problem is solved quickly, the decision process requires countless neural connections.

The understanding of the human brain has improved drastically over the past century, and new theories of logic have made it possible for analysis of logical thought to improve the way humans think. Comprehending the ways your brain functions can change the way you learn, overall improving your way of life.

Logical Thinking

Logical thinking involves two distinct forms of thinking, often referred to as inductive and deductive reasoning. The difference between the two comes from the order of reasoning and solid evidence or observations made. Both forms of logical thinking involve judgment on either ideas or observations. These conclusions are based on objective reality, since neither form of logical thinking provides conclusive evidence without proof.

Inductive Reasoning

Inductive reasoning is based on observation. For example, if you had a box full of many objects, but you did not know what was inside, a first step might be to remove one object at a time. When you pull out ten or more bouncy balls, you may conclude that the box is full of bouncy balls. Induction moves from a process of observation, to detection of patterns, to a hypothesis, to a theory.

One of the most popular examples of inductive reasoning comes in the form of Sherlock Holmes. In one of Sir Arthur Conan Doyle's favorite works, "A Scandal in Bohemia," Holmes is hired to find the location of a photograph of Irene Adler for the next king of Bohemia. Through induction, he is able to infer that the photographs and letters are not on her person since she is slim and cannot hide them.

He and John Watson head to her apartment and find her in the street, walking casually. Holmes and Watson appear to have a scuffle in which Holmes is hurt when he fights for her honor. Irene takes him to her apartment to recover. The two detectives' instigate a plan to make her believe that there is a fire in her building, ultimately causing her to run to her most prized possession: the photograph of the king.

Holmes used inductive reasoning to procure the photograph by using observation to develop a theory of its location. His observation of her person and basic human tendencies to keep valuable items close led him to discover her photograph.

Qualitative research, which is the study of underlying patterns based on the quality of observations, is one of the most commonly used in inductive reasoning. Investigations mainly focus on small sample groups. In the story "A Scandal in Bohemia," Holmes used only Irene Adler as his focus of study. The study of other individuals, though providing a unique look into how Irene would react, was second to his observation of her.

Deductive Reasoning

The other most common form of reasoning is in the form of deductive reasoning. The deductive reasoning process is opposite to inductive reasoning. In this case, thought precedes observation. For example, the statements "Cats meow; Arlene is a cat; Arlene meows" follows the thought process of deductive reasoning. Theory suggests that all cats meow, so, if Arlene is a cat, she must meow, which leads to observation and a definitive conclusion.

Aristotle's famous sea battle example illustrates the process of deductive reasoning. He states that just because there is a possibility for a sea battle tomorrow does not necessarily guarantee it occurring. The theory that there will be a sea battle tomorrow is justified by observation of tomorrow's defenses.

Aristotle taught that a theory must be proved to conclude deductive reasoning. This form of reasoning is extremely common in science today. One of the most influential theories came through the theory of quantum particles. Many mathematical claims suggested that quantum particles existed. Theories created as far back as 480 B.C. theorized their existence. Since then, many determined that there must be particles smaller than those found in molecules. After all, since molecules are different, there must be smaller elements that make up these molecules.

Electron behavior was first observed by J.J. Thomson by using cathode ray tubes which sent a charge through a vacuum. He observed the behavior and developed his own theory after the observation. Though this theory would also prove lacking, the initial theory of atom behavior provided a basis for future experiments.

Deductive reasoning is based on quantitative research. Quantitative takes large value sets and develops a statistical basis as evidence. A scientific theory must be tested multiple times before it is considered correct, which ultimately supports the theory. Deductive research is a cycle of questions and answers. The theory is the question posed, and many qualitative experiments either agree or disagree with the theory.

Traditional Brain Function Theories

No doubt you have heard about the split brain explanation. It is one of the most common theories in play today, though it was suggested around 150 years ago. In a study done on two men that had brain damage on the right hemisphere, scientists of the day concluded that language must be something that originates on the left side of the brain.

As the theory became more popular, writers began to expound on the subject, stating that the left side of the brain is responsible for logic while the right side is more focused on creativity. The new explanation for which sides of the brain control logic and creativity became the standard theory for brain functions.

In 1981, Joseph Bogen, Robert Ornstein, and Roger Sperry received the Nobel Prize for coming up with this method of splitting the brains into two sides. They experimented on patients who supposedly had issues with either side of the brain, usually due to strokes or epilepsy. They found that the side of the brain most affected showed reduced signs of either logic or creativity, spawning the theory.

The left side of the brain is often considered the logical side. If you listen to the hype about the split brain theory, you will notice that people who claim to be dominantly left-brained are more practical, logical, factual, and a host of other similar characteristics. Left-brained people are often in mathematical fields such as engineering or architecture. They break information down into the facts and have difficulty creating.

People with right-brained personalities are more creative. They exhibit a knack for painting, writing, and are generally more imaginative than people with left-brained personalities. These people go into fields like language studies, social studies, and art, just to name a few. These people find their passion in learning visually and orally and have difficulty grasping logical subjects like math.

Neuroscientific Evidence

Despite popular belief, recent evidence has shown the split brain theory incorrect. Though it is true that the left hemisphere plays a large part in language, one side of the brain does not work independently of the other.

There are two hemispheres of the brain as seen from the surface area. When dissecting the brain, many internal regions are made of the same tissue, separated into left and right portions. However, internal parts of the brain are linked together. The striatum, hypothalamus, thalamus, and brain stem are just some of these internal regions. The left and right regions do control separate parts of the body like movement and eyesight.

The brain is not perfectly symmetrical. In fact, the top right side of the brain is slightly larger than the left, and the back left part of the brain is slightly bigger than the right. Iain McGilchrist suggests that the brain looks as though it has been twisted slightly, creating space for the larger parts of the brain. The brain is located in a symmetrical skull, and the rest of the body. There must be some reason for this differentiation.

Humans are not the only beings to have this feature. All creatures have some variation of this asymmetrical brain configuration for the same reasons: a difference of attention. The right and left parts of the brain control the opposite sides of the body. For example, the right hemisphere tells the left arm to raise and vice versa. One of the reasons for this dates back millennia. When humans were hunters and gatherers, they required quick reflexes. So, if a predator was seen from the right, the body would jump to the left. This reflex could mean the difference between life and death in the wild.

Though this is not as important today as we generally do not need to dodge predators, it is still possible to see how part of the brain is affected by viewing the body. You may notice that someone who suffers from a stroke sometimes loses temporary or permanent control of one side of his or her body, the opposite of where the injury occurred in the brain.

Consider the logic of two separate sides of the brain working against each other. It does not make sense that one side of the brain would shut off when the other side is activated. Musicians have a key sense of mathematics. Why? They use rhythm and patterns to solve problems musically. Both sides of the brain must work together to make sense of a problem.

This suggests that emotions, creativity, and logical thinking are more deeply connected than science originally theorized. The right side of the brain is devoted to risk taking, flexibility, and accepting change. The left side of the brain keeps the right in check. Without the left hemisphere, people would not be able to complete their dreams. There is a necessary rigidity to accomplishing goals. Essentially, the right side of the brain is responsible for the larger issues while the left side of the brain is more focused.

Creativity comes down to balance. The brain separates its tasks between the two, giving an example such as this: "Interest (left and right), preparation (left), incubation (right), illumination (right), verification (left) application (left and right). It is a balanced process-- four 'lefts' and four 'rights'" (Herrmann, 1998). This is essentially the creative process.

However, the frontal lobe is responsible for reining in both sides of the brain. This is useful to both empathize with others and to deceive them. Scrutiny comes from correctly separating the intentions and emotions of others by inhibiting your own focus. Consider viewing something either very close or very far away. Either way, you cannot see properly. You must have a separation of mind to both scrutinize others while still seeing the bigger picture.

The left hemisphere is responsible for Machiavellian thought. It is what leads us to manipulate the world. Manipulation is necessary to survive in the world. We manipulate the tools used to grow food. We manipulate our own minds by forcing concentration. The left hemisphere is the one most often considered the best of the two hemispheres because it allows for careful analysis of information.

The right side of the brain is responsible for intuition. It is the right side of the brain makes the world relatable. Mental illnesses pop up in the world due to humans' needs to control the world about them. The right hemisphere allows for thoughts that do not depend on the careful scrutiny of life, thus freeing the mind.

Brain Functions

Though there is a large amount of data we do have of how the brain functions, there is still much more unknown. The brain is highly complex, which makes it difficult to map, even with brain imaging systems. Some believe that reasoning is deeply flawed by the interactions between the two hemispheres, while others believe that the brain uses these differences in logic to create new information, thus leading to correct resolutions.

Neuroimagery

Experts have concluded that one of the best times to determine brain function is during developmental stages. If we understand the way the brain works when it is developing, we can better understand why people reason the way they do. However, it is often difficult to find subjects in tender ages to test. Understandably, the risks make many parents nervous. However, there are a few noninvasive methods scientists use to study the brain.

The first is electroencephalography (EEG), which attaches electrodes to the head and determines what electrical pulses are activated when thinking. It is commonly used because it is able to detect electrical impulses precisely. However, EEG scans are often unspecific: they do not accurately depict where the electrical impulses take place. Thus, it is difficult to determine how these electrical impulses affect the brain.

Magnetoencephalography (MEG) is far superior to EEG scans when it comes to understanding which parts of the brain are used in brain activity. Magnetic waves are perpendicular to electric ways, making changes in electric fields easier to identify. MEG scans are less likely to be affected by the skull, which means that it is much easier to map the brain with these types of scans. However, MEG scans suffer from changes in sound. Even when participants move, the change in vibrations severely affects the efficiency of the scans.

One of the most common forms of brain scans is in the form of magnetic resonance imagery (MRI). These scans make mapping the brain much easier. They accurately depict the brain in terms of gray matter and neural pathways. However, they are often not as efficient as either EEG or MEG scans in determining the electrical impulses in the brain. They also pose a problem when viewing children's brains since the participant must hold still. However, MRI is still a go-to for scientists when mapping the brain.

Heterogenous Cerebral Network

Today, we know that the brain is highly specialized. Each section of the brain is responsible for a certain task. For example, the hippocampus is responsible for emotions, memory and learning. The thalamus detects sensations such as temperature and touch.

One of the most common theories in brain activity today centers around a hierarchy. Some of the brain's functions are more prominent than others. The procedures to measure these reactions come from electrical impulses in the mind. MEG scans show where brain spikes occur and their intensity.

When expressing emotion, a participant shows spikes in the hippocampus, though the areas affected vary. The hippocampus does not simply light up when emotion is expressed; small portions of it show more activity than others. The brain exhibits different spikes for sadness and happiness, though both emotions are based in the hippocampus.

Imagine setting up a task to complete a highly complex philosophical question. The use of emotions is essential in differentiating the moral aspects of the solution. Utilizing proper language when understanding and communicating the problem and result help to both examine the meaning of the problem and disclose it effectively. Learning about yourself and those around you affect the way you see the world.

The answer is depicted through the use of all sections of the brain and their communication. The list above is highly simplistic. The connections between each section of the brain may bounce around to different portions of the brain before ultimately reaching a decision.

All areas of the brain communicate with each other through neural impulses, so categorizing spikes in the brain helps it cope with cognitive function. The brain is highly task-dependent, separating impulses to compartmentalize difficult thoughts. Reasoning, therefore, requires the use of all sections of the brain, though spikes occur at different times to not overwhelm the brain.

The brain is ultimately responsible for making connections. After all, that is what logic is, the ability to separate what makes sense. Without these connections, reasoning is not possible. For example, without the thalamus, pain could not be sent to the cerebral cortex, which is responsible for interpreting the message. Without the connection between the posterior parietal cortex and prefrontal cortex, the brain could not understand mathematics. The combination of electrical impulses of the brain make reasoning possible.

Chapter 2:

The Principles of Logic

It is said that the ancient Greek philosopher Parmenides discovered logic when he sat on a rock in Egypt. Of course, the legend is likely inaccurate, but Parmenides was still one of the first people to develop the concept of logic. Instead of merely citing visual evidence, he created arguments for subjects using thought. He is the first to exhibit signs of critical thinking.

The principles of logic pertain to most forms of understanding. Without these principles, human logic would not exist. Though simple, understanding the principles of logic makes critical thinking easier.

Three Laws of Logic

Aristotle is considered the father of logic. He believed that, though an abstract solution may exist, it must be backed by proof, thus forcing a logical explanation. Though he was not the first to require proof to win a debate, he broke down thought processes into distinctive laws, often called the three laws of logic.

These laws are the 1) the law of noncontradiction, 2) the law of excluded middle, and 3) the principle of identity.

The Law of Noncontradiction

There are arguably three cases of the law of noncontradiction, ontological, doxical, and semantic. The first relates to what we see, the second to what we believe, and the third to truth. Without these three laws of noncontradiction, we presumably would not know anything about the world today.

In layman's terms, the law of noncontradiction for ontological logic states that one cannot be defined as two variations of a linguistic expression. For example, someone cannot be a pitcher for a baseball team and be a pitcher that pours beverages. The same language does not mean that an object must be both types of pitchers. Logic states that the person must be one or the other. So, x may be A and could not be A, but A cannot both be A and not be A.

The law of noncontradiction for doxical logic states that one cannot believe and disbelieve a concept. For example, many politicians today claim that they both believe a subject and yet find instances in which it does not apply. Logically, you cannot believe A and not believe A at the same time. This type of logic is often highly disputed because humans are naturally contradictory. They may believe something at one point in time and deny it later. Philosophical thinkers are still trying to break down this kind of logic.

Aristotle also claims that it is not possible for someone to believe something that defies rationality, following doxical logic. So, he might claim that atoms exist because there is empirical evidence of their existence. However, this type of doxical logic also falls into dangerous territory since many things that were once thought correct were discounted later.

The semantic logic approach is sometimes viewed as a continuation of the first. It states that two contrary ideas cannot be right at the same time. In essence, A cannot equal B if they contradict. Logic assumes that there is only one right answer. This type of logic is common in scientific fields, since evidence and mathematical reason can often only reach one correct conclusion.

The Law of Excluded Middle

The law of excluded middle states that there is no middle ground between truth and falsehood. Essentially, a statement is either correct, or it is not. For many, this absolute nature is unsettling. Surely there must be a compromise. However, in many cases, there is simply a statement of fact and one of opinion, and one is correct. Critical thinking forces one to think about what makes sense, which is the essence of logic.

This law is often subject to controversy, especially to those who do not have facts to back up their claims or the time needed to investigate further. Many believe that there is not one right or wrong answer, but in most cases, facts do not support that theory.

The Principle of Identity

Perhaps the most obvious of principles states that A is equal to itself. This may seem redundant, but it holds a philosophical meaning that is deeper. Without understanding the identity of a person or an object, it is impossible to determine unique characteristics. For example, we may say that a table is red and that it cannot be anything other than red. We may also say that a person exists in a world populated by nearly 8 billion people, which defines a unique trait.

An object defined cements its place in the universe. Its existence is a matter of fact. René Descartes coined the popular phrase, "I think, therefore I am." This suggests that the world could not exist without the identity of thinkers. The principle of identity suggests that the universe would not exist without thought.

The Fundamentals of the Logical/Critical Thinking Process

Everyone has the innate ability to think critically. However, it is now common to take opinion as fact, accepting fake news and biased information that discounts logic. To understand how to think critically, you must understand how the critical thinking process works.

The Nine Rules of Thinking Critically

To think logically, one must follow a set of guidelines. When first learning to think logically, you may already notice that your mind forms rational conclusions. That is the first step to thinking logically. However, someone who can think critically must be thorough to come to correct conclusions. Follow these basic rules of logic to develop your critical thinking skills.

1. *Gather Information*:

Critical thinkers gather all the information they need before reaching a conclusion. This includes all sides of an argument. Coming to the conclusion that veganism is the best diet for the body requires an analysis of meat and meatless diets. Only then can you come to a rational conclusion.

It is not enough to simply find information that is easily accessible. Because there are many incorrect sources on the internet, you must gather information from multiple sources and compare the results. Many sources try to sell products, drawing many away with false conclusions.

You may find the best way to gather information is to conduct your own experiments. Ultimately, this is one of the best ways to determine correct information. If you feel better on a vegan diet and are getting all the minerals and vitamins needed, you may conclude that a vegan diet is the best form of diet.

2. _Understand All Terminology_:

When gathering information, be sure to understand the terminology. You cannot correctly judge information without being able to define all the terms in your own words. Also, define the parameters of the information. Understand how researchers reached their conclusions.

3. _Question Methods, Conclusions, and Sources_:

A common admonition states, "Don't believe everything you read." An iconic example comes from the story of the Russian princess Anastasia Romanov. When a child, she was spirited and a prankster, easily loved by the public. She was the most outgoing of her siblings, making her more relatable. When the Russian revolution began, Lenin's men took the Romanov family from their home and lined them up in a cellar. Each member was shot and buried in an unknown location.

Many years later, a woman in Germany was pulled from a ditch and put into a mental institution. Her features bore a resemblance to the princess Anastasia, and she hardly dismissed the claims. Soon, rumors started to arise stating that the princess had been carried, unconscious, away from the scene while the rest of her family was buried. The woman known as Anna Anderson neither confirmed nor denied this theory, making speculation spread further.

Gleb Botkin, whose father was a physician for the royal family and was killed with them, had no doubt in his mind that Anna Anderson was the princess of Russia. He claimed he knew who she was from sight, as he had seen Anastasia many times as a child. He became one of her most ardent supporters, claiming that his relationship with Anderson was based on the interactions he had had with her when she was a child.

Recently, DNA testing has shown that Anna Anderson was not related to the Romanovs, and Anastasia's body has been exhumed with the rest of her family. The speculation started from a resemblance with no facts. However, the story of Anna Anderson created a phenomenon that has inspired movies and musicals for years.

If nothing else, this story explains the lack of critical thought. Many wanted to believe in a fairytale, but there was no evidence to support it. Even the source Botkin did not know Anderson's true identity, though he claimed to have known her from the start. Thinking critically means to doubt the evidence until it is proven correct.

4. *Look for Biases and Assumptions*:

Scientific computation dictates that there should be little to no bias when conducting an experiment. When critical thinking, do not let biases and assumptions skew the truth. Biases such as race, religion, political opinion, and many others can influence the truth, making conducted research obsolete.

Once you have reached a conclusion, identify which biases and assumptions affect your conclusion. One way to do this is to play the devil's advocate. What would the other party say when doing the same research? Develop an objective opinion by arguing for all sides of the issue.

5. _Expect Limited Answers_:

In many cases, there is not enough evidence to fully support one theory over another. The big bang theory states that the universe was created some 13 billion years ago from an explosion that contained all the matter in the universe. This theory is supported by evidence of the expanding universe and corroborates with theories about the four forces in the universe.

However, since there is no direct evidence showing that is exactly what happened, it is very difficult, if not impossible, to determine if this theory is correct. There were no sources at the time of the big bang, and observation can only take us so far in discovering the truth.

6. _Consider the Bigger Picture_:

It is easy to get lost in the details when examining a problem, but the best way to come to a conclusion is to consider the bigger picture. Think about looking into a microscope at a golf ball. If you zoom in by a factor of 100, it becomes difficult to see what the object is. The details of the golf ball make up the whole, but it is not until you zoom out that you understand what you are seeing.

Consider the logic of an argument by taking the information you have gathered and combining it to give a final theory. In most cases, the evidence supports a wider explanation.

7. *Examine Cause and Effect*:

If *A* occurs, then it leads to *B*. This part of reasoning is what leads to conclusive arguments. For example, when a boy broke his arm, the doctor put on a cast. If the boy had not broken his arm, there would be no need for the cast. The laws of cause and effect help us view patterns from observation.

To truly understand a difficult subject, it may be necessary to examine evidence that shows similar cause and effect patterns. If you are located in a desert, you may not know that the accumulation of snow and rain causes rivers to swell every year. However, using the right materials, you can see the evidence for yourself.

8. *Maintain Thought*:

One of the most common thought stoppers is doubt. Though it is important to use doubt to come to a viable conclusion, self-doubt can make it difficult to continue thinking critically. Maintain thought by continuing to find evidence. Do not let your thoughts or impressions prevent you from thinking logically.

Another type of thought stopper is accepting an answer before you have researched completely. Many people use manipulative tactics to persuade you to think one way or another. For example, someone stating that you do not care for women if you do not support abortion, it is common to fall into a trap of fear. Rationally come to conclusions despite opposition.

9. *Understand Yourself*:

If you have a predisposition to one side of an argument, understand that you must develop your argument for all sides. Hot button topics such as abortion or gun control are often the most common ways to discover what your biases are. Discover the benefits and disadvantages to your point of view.

Critical Thinking Abilities

Though there are many ways to think logically, everyone thinks with nine types of abilities, namely observational, emotional, questioning, imaginative, inferential, experimenting, consulting, argument, or judgment skills. That is not to say that you are predisposed to use only one of these abilities. However, the majority of people prefer one method to another.

1. *Observational Abilities*:

One of the most common types of critical thinking abilities is observational. Detectives such as Sherlock Holmes were able to draw conclusions from the evidence. In fact, those who enter the police force generally have a higher ability to find clues from looking at photographs.

Observational critical thinkers are able to use their abilities to decipher what makes a scene less than trustworthy. This may include smelling, seeing, touching, tasting, or hearing out of the ordinary.

Observational abilities are also common in calculations. People with these abilities can spot what makes a calculation incorrect by reviewing previous work.

2. *Emotional Abilities*:

This ability is innate and is most commonly viewed in children. When was the last time you noticed a child experimenting with something to see what happened? Children have a natural curiosity that guides them to think critically. Unfortunately, many schools stifle this ability by giving answers and not stimulating a child's sense of curiosity. That does not mean that you do not still have this ability. It simply takes time and motivation to return to your naturally curious state.

3. *Questioning Abilities*:

Children are also naturally predisposed to questioning, just ask any four-year-old. However, questioning abilities in critical thinking are more advanced. Someone gifted with these abilities can form a clear question out of rudimentary information, foregoing any unclear language or logic.

Some of the greatest scientists in history have had this ability. Sir Isaac Newton asked why an apple fell and developed a theory for gravity. Galileo Galilei dropped two spheres of different masses from the leaning tower of Pisa to determine if they hit the ground at separate times. Eratosthenes questioned if the world was round before performing an experiment with two towers and their shadows to determine not only its shape but its circumference. Great thinkers question the world around them as a form of critical thinking, driving their goals to understand.

4. *Imaginative Abilities*:

Thinking critically involves imagination. Consider architecture: an architect must not only develop a beautiful building, but it must have functions appropriate for human living. For example, if you were to develop a building to function on Mars, where would you start? You may consider adding a decontamination chamber to clean people and restore oxygen levels. You may consider adding plants to your base to create a continual supply of breathable air. These solutions are the results of imagination.

Critical thinking is not just finding solutions to questions by developing what you have, but it involves an inventive nature. Many scientists ask what could make their theories better and more straightforward to develop their thought processes and make sense of the world.

5. *Inferential Abilities*:

Consider the following example: A woman comes home from a camping trip and itches from head to foot. She had been wearing a long shirt and pants and had hiking boots on. She does not show any indication of bumps, only the presence of occasional rashes on her body. What might be the reason for this?

Someone with a predisposition for inferential abilities would infer, based on the evidence, that she had an allergic reaction to some food. Why? She does not show any bumps, which might indicate bug bites. She wore full clothing, which squashes the possibility that she rubbed up against poison oak or another plant that might induce rashes. One of the only possibilities left is an allergic reaction to food.

People with inferential abilities can determine an outcome based on evidence. This ability is often paired with others, such as observation or emotion. To infer, you must analyze any possible solutions and develop a response that would justify the answer.

6. _Experimenting Abilities_:

Though everyone has the ability to experiment, only some have an innate sense of asking the right questions to create an experiment that will answer questions effectively. People with experimenting abilities develop the right sample sizes, are highly specific with theories, and develop excellent experiment designs.

Someone without this ability has problems narrowing down factors. For example, a professor wants to experiment with the effectiveness of footwear on harsh surfaces. She chooses 100 types of shoes, and has a student walk on glass, nails, and coals. This experiment does not narrow down the type of shoes tested, what kind of harsh surfaces, or the results she expects to be produced. The experiment is faulty.

7. _Consulting Abilities_:

People with consulting abilities both ask the right questions and can differentiate between true and faulty information. These people are able to determine which types of information are necessary and how to narrow down what they find.

    8.   *Argument Analysis Abilities*:

Arguments are composed of premises and conclusions, and understanding the language of these premises lead to a logical conclusion. People with argument analysis abilities can break down information and determine if it is valid or not, leading to an accurate conclusion. More about arguments will be mentioned later.

    9.   *Judging and Deciding Abilities*:

Judging and deciding skills are essentially a part of the inferring abilities listed above. People with this ability can differentiate between logical and illogical information, ultimately leading to a logical conclusion.

Reason Logically

Now, suppose you are stuck in a jungle after being separated from your group which was looking for ancient Aztec civilizations. You are hopelessly lost, and the jungle is making it difficult for you to get your bearings. Since you believed that you would only be on this expedition for only a few hours, you did not bother to bring more than a small water bottle and no food.

While you are making your way through the jungle, you recognize some mushrooms that might or might not be edible. In most cases, it is difficult to differentiate the good mushrooms for the bad, and eating a poisonous mushroom could make you sick or even kill you. So, what do you do?

An irrational person may decide to eat the mushrooms simply because he or she is hungry, but you are trying to think critically. You have heard that you should not eat a mushroom unless you are positive that it will not hurt you. However, there are over 10,000 species of mushroom, and your college major was psychology, so you are not an expert in the subject.

You have heard that there are edible mushrooms in the jungle, but you do not know how to identify them. You decide to test the mushrooms by watching to see if an animal eats them first. A lemur decides to take a mushroom in passing, but you see it disappear into the jungle, so you are not able to determine if the animal suffered or not. The only sure way to know if they are edible or not is to eat one. However, as a critical thinker, you realize that the potential issues outweigh the potential benefits and move on.

The example above follows the reasoning process to bring you to a logical conclusion. A logical thinker does not make moves on a whim but experiments to improve the chances of getting the right answer.

Rational thinking and reasoning is the acceptance of the knowledge that you do not know the answer to a problem. If you accept that there is no other explanation for an object or occurrence, critical thinking ends. So, there must be some element of doubt that prevents you from settling on one conclusion.

The reason for critical thinking usually falls into three possible explanations: 1) to determine what to believe, 2) to prove the accuracy of a preconceived notion, and 3) to practice critical thinking that is on the same threshold as the original claim. A critical thinker uses all three instances to better understand a concept or to solve a problem. In all, a logical thinker is extremely goal oriented.

Developing Arguments

Reasoning is developed through premises and conclusions. Premises are stipulations that, if proven true, lead to a logical conclusion. Consider, for example, the premises listed below.

Dogs are mammals.

Max is a dog.

Therefore, Max is a mammal.

Logically, we must conclude that the final statement is correct if the first two sentences, the premises, dictate so. The basis of Aristotle's three laws of logic explain that, if premises are correct, we can come to a relevant conclusion.

However, there are instances when a premise is correct, but the conclusion is either incorrect or is not necessarily true, which is called a counterexample. For example, the premise "The weatherman said it was going to rain this afternoon" may cause many to conclude that it will rain. However, just because the weatherman said it was true does not mean that it will rain. It also does not mean that the weatherman is lying when he predicts the conclusion. The argument falls apart with the simple statement, "They could be wrong."

Critical thinkers determine the likelihood of a conclusion by analyzing the probability of its success. The example given about Max the dog is easily proved truthful because of previous experimentation and definitive language. Max is a dog, therefore, he is a mammal. However, the counterexample is based on evidence that is subject to change. Though we have improved information and technology that can predict the weather, there is no way to guarantee, 100%, that it will rain.

Good and Bad Arguments

Arguments are generally divided into two categories: sound and unsound. Sound arguments prove without a shadow of a doubt that the conclusion is correct. Unsound arguments, though occasionally possessing truthful statements, cannot be proven indefinitely.

Logic is only based on the possibility of absolute truth, not if a statement may be true in some instances.

There are two stipulations that lead to a sound argument: 1) an argument must be factually correct to reach a logical conclusion, and 2) an argument must follow its premises to be considered valid. If both of these contingencies are met, the argument is sound. All statements *must* be correct for this to be allowed.

Consider this example:

> All wild animals are dangerous.
>
> Dogs are not wild animals.
>
> Dogs are not dangerous.

Though it is entirely possible that many dogs are not dangerous, there are some domesticated dogs that do cause harm. This argument is not sound because of the underlying "what if?" The counterexample would suggest that some domesticated dogs have been abused and exhibit aggressive tendencies. Therefore, this logic is unsound.

Consider a set of premises and a conclusion regarding Alex.

> All mathematicians are intelligent.
>
> Alex is not a mathematician.
>
> Alex is not intelligent.

How sound is this logic? Can we resolutely determine that Alex is not intelligent because he is not a mathematician? These statements provide a counterexample. Alex does not need to be a mathematician to be intelligent. The two are not mutually exclusive. This means that one statement does not rely on the other to be correct.

Now, consider another set of premises and a conclusion.

All animal haters are stupid.

Heather hates animals.

Heather is stupid.

Is this a counterexample? To find the answer, we must determine if there are any issues on the premises. In essence, is there a way we can say there is reasonable doubt in proclaiming Heather stupid? This is not a counterexample. The premises lead to a logical conclusion, even if the argument is a bad one.

Chapter 3:

Is Your Brain Holding You

Back?

One of the most common causes of failure in critical thinking is allowing yourself to believe that either you have all the answers or you only look for the information that supports your claim. This type of behavior stops critical thinking and pushes you back into old habits, relying on yourself to answer questions you may not know the answers to.

Cognitive Bias

To think critically, you must analyze your own thoughts. What perceived biases do you have toward the subject you are researching? You may feel a moral obligation to find answers to support your claim, or you may simply want to win an argument. You may not even be aware of the bias that is preventing you from receiving a logical result. So, whenever you presume yourself to be right, question your desires.

Cognitive bias is a systematic error. This means that there is something wrong with the way you approach thought. Cognitive bias is nothing new; it affects the way we make decisions and come to conclusions on a daily basis. Something as small as viewing a happy child can affect your thoughts toward a neighborhood playground. The best way to overcome cognitive bias is to recognize it, and there are several forms.

Confirmation Bias

When was the last time you tried to win an argument? Chances are that, if you are highly invested in the subject, you found evidence that backed up your claim and disregarded the other information. This is confirmation bias and is common when defending or opposing hot button topics.

One example comes in the form of gun control. If you are in favor of gun control, you would find evidence that supports the theory that guns in the hands of citizens puts people at unnecessary risk. If you are not in favor of gun control, you may find stories and information about how guns have saved lives. There is plenty of data to back up both sides of the argument. The bias lies in which evidence is more sought after.

Another form of confirmation bias occurs when you observe an action and change evidence to support your belief. For example, if you text a friend and he does not respond after several hours, you may assume that he is trying to avoid you. Every text message you receive after this seems like an excuse from your friend to throw you off the scent. Soon, you start acting on this belief.

People who have anxiety or have been subjected to bad behavior in the past are most likely to have confirmation bias. They observe what they perceive to be patterns of wrongdoing and play on it. For example, if a woman has been abused in the past, she may perceive gift-giving as an attempt to win her favor and control her. A man with anorexia may think that anyone attempting to give him high-calorie foods is trying to control his body.

Confirmation bias is like a drug since it is so easy to get emotional about beliefs. The more others try to contradict your ideas, the easier it becomes to be irrational in your responses. Confirmation bias causes you to stop gathering information as soon as you have reached a conclusion. It is easier to assume that every piece of evidence following substantiating evidence is either wrong or flawed. Critical thinkers, however, gather evidence from all sides of the story.

Hindsight Bias

When was the last time you looked back at an event and thought, "I know that was going to happen?" Hindsight bias affects the way we perceive patterns that occurred in the past. For example, in a college psychology experiment, students were asked if they believed that Clarence Thomas would be elected to the U.S. supreme court. When asked before the election, 58% of students believed that she would. After the election, students were asked the same question. A whopping 78% of students said that they knew she would be elected (Cherry, 2020a). Students were more likely to admit that they saw a pattern after the experiment concluded.

Of course, this type of bias is popular in other fields as well. How many times did you get a test back and exclaim, "I knew the answer to that one!" when in fact the answer was marked incorrect? It is natural for people to believe that they knew the outcome before an event occurred. Researchers suggest that there are three levels of hindsight bias: 1) memory manipulation, 2) inevitability, and 3) foreseeability. These levels range from simple distortion to near-awareness.

The first case is memory manipulation or misremembering. Imagine a car crash taking the lives of two people. You remember that a semi-truck slammed into the side of a car, which killed the driver and passenger. In your mind, the semi-truck driver is at fault. However, security cameras show that the car was passing through a red light when the truck slammed into them. You remembered correctly, but you did not remember all the factors.

The second level is inevitability. Back in 2008 when Barack Obama was sworn in as the president of the United States, many said, "It had to happen eventually." They believed that it was only a matter of time before a black president was sworn in. However, at the time of the election, many of these people did not believe he would become the president. These people deluded themselves into thinking that they were right all along.

The final level is foreseeability. This is the highest level of hindsight bias because it assumes that the observer could have seen the events unfolding before they occurred. Usually, this occurs when basing results on firmly-held beliefs. In either case, there is no guarantee of success, but hindsight bias insists that the event was foreseeable.

To prevent hindsight bias, examine how you came to this conclusion. One of the most difficult parts to overcome is the belief in your ability to forecast the future. Once you accept other explanations, you become more open to critical thinking. Confidence in your own ability is one of the most common ways this occurs.

Anchoring Bias

The anchoring bias refers to the bias related to the first piece of information you hear. If I say there are around 32 countries in Europe, what would your final guess be? If you guess a number close to the one I suggested and not 44, which is the correct number, you may be experiencing anchoring bias.

This can also extend to arbitrary numbers. A study by Tversky and Kahneman discovered that spinning a number between 0 and 100 affected the way participants guessed how many countries are in Africa.

If the participant spun a large number, he or she guessed a higher number, and the same applied to those who spun a low number (Cherry, 2020c). Hearing any data before the critical thinking process affects the outcome.

You will also likely see anchoring bias affect you even from a young age. If you were raised to believe that you could only watch television for one hour every day, you will tend to believe that any more time might be unhealthy. If you searched online for a car and found that it was commonly sold for $25,000, you may feel ecstatic when you find one for $23,500, even though the same car is sold for $20,000 across town.

To avoid this bias, do research. The anchoring bias is hard to overcome, but if you have a solid basis of information, you can start thinking critically. Doctors ask questions to their patients even though they have a record in front of them to prevent anchoring bias. Before you settle on data, develop your own thoughts of what should be accurate.

The Misinformation Effect

Not only can our minds be influenced by remembering incorrectly, but they can also be changed by subtle influences. Imagine spending a night out with your friends. You may have remembered going to see the movie *The Commuter*, but a friend tells you that you went to see *Singin' in the Rain*. Even if you did see the former, you may believe that you saw the latter, following the friend's suggestion.

Researchers have also used subtle language differences to influence the way people reacted to their memories. In a study done by Elizabeth Loftus, she asked participants to view a video of crashing cars. After a week, she asked one group how fast the cars were going when they either *hit* each other or *smashed into* each other. These subtle differences yielded different results when asked if they saw glass on the scene. Those in the latter group claimed they had, though there was no broken glass.

There are many theories that attempt to discover why the misinformation effect occurs. One states that the use of language and other subtle influences causes the brain to become confused and ultimately blends the two memories together. The misinformation effect is usually not a form of deception, so the brain does not think twice when assigning new information.

Another theory suggests that the memory is permanently changed. Some theorists speculate that no memories are the same as when first experienced. Every time you review them in your head, you make slight alterations. Therefore, every memory is rewritten after you remember it once. This is a popular opinion since it is possible to alter your perception of a bad day to make it worse by adding slight effects such as rain. Even if you experienced a sunny day when you were stuck inside with a cold, the brain adds a different element to the memory.

Other researchers believe that retrieving new memories is easier than old memories. So, if someone suggests an alteration to your memory, it is easier to retrieve the alteration than it is to delve back further. Since the brain links together with neural connections, retrieving old memories may demand more work.

There are a number of factors that play into misinformation. Time is often distorted in memories. When remembering events years prior, the time distortion can make it seem like a dream. You see bits and pieces of events, but it is mixed together to seem like fluid motion. News reports are also common culprits for distortion. News people are generally considered trustworthy, which can make you doubt your own memories.

To combat the misinformation effect, think critically about events. In most cases, there are instances that do not make logical sense. Do not doubt what you have experienced, and problem-solve with the information you have.

The Actor Observer Bias

Humans tend to create excuses based on outside influences. For example, if you were late for a meeting, you might blame it on the taxi driver, or if you had a bad date, you might blame it on the other person. This type of bias affects the way we view either other people or situations.

This bias is created through previous examples of similar circumstances. If someone was late for a meeting, you would assume that he or she is lazy, just as you have been in the past. It is easier to assign bias to a circumstance or person based on how you or others have acted.

Studies have shown that actor observer bias is less common among people who know each other well. Of course, you know who he or she is, which accounts for his or her behavior.

The False Consensus Effect

The false consensus effect influences your opinion of how many people agree with you. Consider your favorite television show. If you love it, you assume that most others love it as well. It may become difficult to understand others' opinions if you do not share them.

You are more likely to experience this effect when delving into topics that mean a lot to you. Religion and politics are very common entities that affect the way you think other people view them. For example, if you believe that there should be free college tuition for all, you may believe that someone who thinks differently than you is a miser and inconsiderate of others' needs. However, the flip side may insist that free college diminishes its quality.

The false consensus effect occurs because we are often surrounded by people who believe in similar things.

Many grow up in families with distinguished opinions about difficult subjects, so they believe most people think the same way. Social media and news also affect the false consensus effect. Some news stations are more likely to show extreme examples.

Two such examples are the news channels CNN and Fox News. CNN frequently posts stories that side with left-wing politics, while Fox News typically is involved in right-wing stances. Neither of these news channels offer the full truth on any subject. They often only post stories that corroborate with their politics. Therefore, someone who exclusively watches either of these channels would assume that most people share his or her opinions.

A critical thinker navigates the false consensus effect by analyzing both sides of an issue. Usually, there are points advocated for both sides, which discounts the thought that everyone has the same opinions. Since self-esteem is often part of the same opinions, separate yourself from believing that your self-worth is based on your thoughts.

The Halo Effect

David is highly attractive and is a marketer for your company. When your boss calls a meeting between David, Lou, and yourself, he asks for options in securing a greater audience. David suggests that the company introduce a younger audience by introducing cartoons while Lou suggests that the company introduces different products that will appeal to younger audiences. When the boss asks you what you think, you side with David's proposal because he is more attractive.

People who are more attractive or charming are considered more qualified, intelligent, or better suited to a position than others. Think of the last time you interacted with someone you did not know. Were you more likely to judge them kindly if they were charming? This is because your positive emotions toward someone charming or attractive creates positive emotions toward other aspects.

The halo effect was first noted by Edward L. Thorndike who had military officers rank their subordinates. Most officers ranked men according to applied stereotypes that had nothing to do with their overall performance. For example, officers often attributed tall, lean men with hard work and short, overweight men with laziness.

Marketers use the halo effect to persuade customers to buy their products. For example, makeup companies will use famous actresses to endorse eyeshadow to influence you into buying their products. After all, who would not want to look like a beautiful, famous person?

Since the halo effect is so ingrained in society, it is difficult to separate bias from normal thought. The best way to avoid this effect is to view people more objectively. Use your critical thinking skills to determine the validity of arguments before siding with an attractive or charismatic person. In essence, slow down.

The Self-Serving Bias

Just as the name implies, the self-serving bias affects your view of success by assuming you are always in the right. For example, if you get an A on an essay, you tell yourself that you did an excellent job. However, if you get a C, you may start to blame your professor, absolving yourself of blame.

People with depression have a lesser chance of using the self-serving bias. In many cases, the self-serving bias is flipped: they may attribute their success to luck while they blame themselves for receiving a poor result. Of course, people with depression still exhibit the self-serving bias, but it is often to a lesser degree.

To avoid this bias, be aware of your thought process. If you find yourself casting blame, examine the situation and develop a rational thought process. Be aware of the thought process that originally caused you to perceive bias. Often returning to a problem after a few moments of contemplation is enough to resolve the self-serving bias.

Develop a sense of compassion for yourself. If you fail at an increasing rate, take a moment to understand why this is happening. Allowing yourself the option to fail prevents a damaged self-esteem and grants you the opportunity to improve without bringing yourself down. Compassion is also the basis for new self-improving motivation.

The Availability Heuristic

The availability heuristic changes the way you perceive risk by what you have experienced. For example, if you have heard that there are more car jackings in your parents' neighborhood, you may assume that they live in an unsafe place. However, the reason for the increase in car thefts could be related to a passerby, which does not mean that your parents' neighborhood is inherently unsafe.

If you are traveling home for the holidays and you run into traffic that causes several hours of delays, you may avoid going back the way you came. You may have gone this direction hundreds of times in the past, but the bad experience predominantly influences your decision in the future.

Heuristics refers to the way your brain trades off between accuracy and speed. Since your brain is constantly processing an exorbitant amount of data, it is often easier to choose between the two. So, in an effort to speed up the process, your brain sometimes chooses the quick result over critical thinking, which is called the availability heuristic.

Because your mind is using a shortcut to rational thought, it often confuses easy solutions with the truth. So, if you look at social media and see some of your friends posting pictures of themselves on the beach, you may think that you are the only person stuck in a snowstorm back home. In reality, most other people are stuck with you. It is simply easier to believe that everyone is enjoying the weather when no one else posts pictures of being stuck at home.

The availability heuristic also refers to how likely you are to come up with information. In a study conducted by Amos Tversky and David Kahneman, they asked a group of people if it was more common for words to start with the letter *k* than it was if *k* were the third letter of the word. More than double of the subjects stated that there were more words starting with *k*. In actuality, there are far more words with the letter *k* as the third letter of the word. It is easier to think of words that start with *k* than as the third letter because the search for sounds is easier at the beginning of the word.

So, what makes things more available to the brain? In many cases, it depends on the person. For example, if you are a pessimistic person, asking you to come up with five reasons why you are having a terrible year would be easy. However, asking you why this year is good requires more thought. Your predisposition to believe pessimistically affects the way your brain accesses information.

The availability heuristic also plays a part in how we rate ourselves. Studies have shown that people who ride their bikes often are more likely to feel that they do not ride enough than those who ride very little. These people are more able to recall instances when they could have ridden their bikes but did not. The easier it is to retrieve that information, the easier it is to believe that it is correct.

Professors have also used this technique to get better reviews from their students. One professor challenged his students to give him as much criticism as possible. When it became difficult to think of criticism, the students relented that he was a great professor after all. Students gave him an average of 12% higher rating than other classes.

Studies have also shown that simply expecting something to be difficult is enough to persuade someone to not comply. For example, think of one reason that you live in the area that you do. Now, try to think of ten reasons. If you are like most people, you are more likely to find your area more satisfactory if you can think of one reason instead of ten. The added difficulty makes answering this question unsatisfactory.

Things become easier to recall when they are repeated frequently. For instance, you may see more mention of lawyers in your town than seamstresses. Seeing ads and other signs for lawyers may create an illusion that there are more lawyers in your town than there really are. You can make a calculated estimate by determining how frequently you see mention of lawyers.

Unusual events are also often exaggerated. Are you more likely to get struck by lightning or bitten by a shark? Many people would guess that sharks are the greater threat since they are mentioned in the news more frequently and are more unusual than lightning strikes. However, you are 23 times more likely to be hit by lightning than be bitten by a shark. Consider also deaths by botulism and asthma. Since botulism is more unusual than asthma, you may think that they kill roughly the same number of people every year, but asthma is 900 times more lethal than botulism.

The more unusual the events, the more likely people are to guess incorrectly about the frequency. However, comparing similar numbers such as deaths from heart disease and cancer--which is almost a ratio of one to one--is easier to predict than deaths from heart disease and smallpox--which shows that heart disease is 13,000 times more common.

Negative events are also easier to recall than positive events. Imagine finding $100 dollars on your way to work. You were not late for the bus, and you made it to work early. You received a nice note from a coworker that expressed their appreciation for your caring nature. However, at the end of the day, your boss yelled at you for not meeting the sales quota. All of the positive events that occurred during the day had no bearing on the end result: you felt miserable because your boss yelled at you.

However, over the course of a long period of time, positive events are easier to remember. One of the most common examples is the romanticization of the past. The phrase "the good old days" often refers to years, sometimes decades, in the past. People remember the neighbor visits, the time spent outdoors, or the garments worn. They do not remember the threat of measles, corruption in government, or the addiction to drugs.

Vivid imagery is easier to remember, even if the events are unlikely. For example, you may be much more afraid of being eaten by a lion in Africa than you are about contracting a disease from a mosquito. Even though mosquitos are often far more deadly than lions, imagining being chased by a hungry lion is enough to make you break out in sweats.

The Optimism Bias

The optimism bias can be essentially broken down into the phrase, "getting your hopes up." In many cases, it is easy to get your hopes up, especially if you are excited about the future. It is nice to think that something good will happen to us, which is a nice way to look at life, but can ultimately affect the way we behave.

Unfortunately, the optimism bias is difficult to overcome. Even if you recognize it during critical thinking, it is difficult to change your mind. Many try to imagine the worst outcome possible when trying to overcome the optimism bias, but a subconscious part of the mind still focuses on an optimistic result.

Emotions

Emotions are part of what makes us human. We all experience a range of emotions from anger to sadness to happiness to fear, and they are an important part of critical thinking. You do not have to be a Vulcan to think logically. Even Mr. Spock had a wide range of emotions, though they were not at the forefront of his mind. These emotions dictate morality and help you think clearly, within reason.

It is nearly impossible to separate all emotions from critical thinking, and why would you want to? Emotions play a large part in judging correctly. You can often tell the difference between a good and bad decision by that gut feeling. However, the biggest problem that arises from emotions is their overuse.

Think about the last time you had an argument about a friend about something you care about. Was it easy to accept their reasoning, or were you more prone to spout words of anger for his or her opinions? Anger is one of the most difficult emotions to overcome when thinking logically, and it is one of the most important emotions to control.

Fear is another emotion that is often difficult to control and is the basis for anger. Imagine your parents leaving you in the dark when you were a child and afraid. Often, children throw tantrums when they cannot express fear adequately because it is an easy emotional outlet.

There is a reason for this: the blood that normally flows freely in the brain when not under duress is stunted when experiencing fear. The body is thrown into a fight or flight mode that sends the majority of the blood from your head out into your limbs. This is a defense mechanism that saves animals, and was once very important in humans. When a strange sound or uncomfortable situation arose, the mind prepared the body to either put up a fight or flee.

Think of a rabbit as a hawk approaches. It does not think but runs in a zigzag motion, trying to escape the bird. It does not need the use of its brain to tell it where to go, only the use of its limbs to carry it away as fast as possible. The body only has so much energy in reserves and must send it to appropriate locations.

Therefore, if you are afraid, the best way to think critically is to calm yourself down. This often involves deep breaths and careful focus. The brain needs to focus again to perform well. Often, if you are angry, that means you must step away from the situation for a moment before returning.

Sadness changes the chemicals in the brain. Those who suffer from depression are often too bogged down by their own minds that critical thinking is nearly impossible. This is why people who attempt suicide often regret their decisions after they live. The self-preservation instinct is silenced, and it is difficult to return to normal brain functions.

Overcoming sadness is difficult, but it is possible when you take care of yourself. The first step is realizing what you are thinking and allowing your brain to process the situation. In many cases, depressed people suppress emotions and thoughts that make them more miserable. Recognizing these thoughts and emotions help you overcome sadness and think more clearly.

Happiness is perhaps one of the most beneficial emotions when thinking clearly, since your body is often relaxed, allowing your brain to do most of the work. However, being too happy and excited may dull your senses as well. You may not be able to focus on the paths that brought you to a correct conclusion.

The "gut feeling" is another form of emotion that often clouds judgment. Though there are many that advocate for it, intuition ultimately reduces the chances of critical thinking. Those who rely on their instincts often do not pay attention to facts, believing that their guts would not lie to them.

Even when the "gut feeling" ends up incorrect, many provide excuses for the inconsistencies, sometimes claiming that it was the fate of the universe. People who lend themselves too liberally to emotions often use them to explain phenomenon that have nothing to do with them. People who believe in karma like to imagine a world of justice instead of random events in the universe. Relying too much on emotions is usually the basis for illogical thinking.

Advertising and marketing ploys often use emotions to influence you to buy things. For example, when you go into a grocery store, often the first thing you see is the produce, the exciting colors give a sense of freshness and make you happier, therefore, more willing to shop.

Other marketers use fear and anger to influence people. People who are frustrated by snoring may find that they are willing to spend top dollar to prevent either themselves or others from it. Their commercials often include exaggerated snoring noises and images of spouses getting upset. You may sympathize with these people, and your relation draws you in.

Critical Thinking Disposition

Someone's disposition to think critically is based on his or her willingness to go through a logical thought process. Though people may have natural abilities to think clearly, that does not mean that they will naturally resolve to think critically. So, to make critical thinking second nature, you must practice.

Thinking logically means asking basic questions. It is easy to believe that something that is so just is. In essence, it is easy to accept things just as they are without asking questions. Some of the most revolutionary discoveries exist because someone was willing to ask questions about why something behaved the way that it did.

For example, many believed that the sun and the planets revolved around the Earth. It was not until Copernicus suggested that the Earth may revolve around the sun with the other planets that discoveries began happening. Models for the solar system came into existence, and more questions were asked. Critical thinking often means breaking logic down to the core and going further.

Be aware of how you think. Take the time to analyze how you came to a conclusion by breaking down the steps. If any of the steps do not make sense, you are still thinking critically, possibly more so. Frustration is often the precursor to breakthroughs, so do not give up.

After you have come to a conclusion, reverse your thinking. You should be able to arrive at the same result. Mathematicians often use this technique to be sure that their theories are correct. If something is the same backward as it is forward, then it must be correct. When you practice thinking critically, understand how each step in a process affects your end result.

Remember that the brain is prone to using shortcuts to get what it wants. As with the availability heuristic, the brain either chooses fast processing or critical thinking but rarely both. Do not succumb to the quick fix, and your brain will become accustomed to answering the right questions. It does not matter how gifted someone is with thinking critically, if they do not follow the steps, they will not be a master critical thinker.

Chapter 4:

Why We Think Illogically

People are illogical beings. Personal grudges, illogical popular beliefs, and many other causes for this. There are many reasons why we may think illogically. Just look at how the world reacts to everything. People make rash and incorrect decisions all the time. Part of that reason comes from bias, which we discussed in the last chapter. However, knowing how you think illogically will help you recognize a lack of critical thinking in yourself, allowing yourself to grow.

Cynicism

To the ancient Greeks, cynicism meant something completely different than it does today. Cynics rejected all forms of modern technology and often lived like dogs in the street, eating raw meat and sleeping in bare shelters. Today, however, that definition has changed slightly. Cynics still reject thought, but they do not live in its perpetual rejection.

Cynicism is often mistaken for critical thinking. If you have doubts about a belief or practice, then you are cynical about it. However, cynicism has gone too far. Where critical thinkers question statements and beliefs, they also open to accepting new ideas. Cynics are obstinate and refuse to progress, thinking they have reached the ultimate form of thought.

Studies have shown that cynical people are not rated as the most competent individual in their fields, but there is a reason the myth connecting cynicism with intelligence has endured. People are taught to survive our surroundings. The phrase "dog-eat-dog world" is common because people believe that they must only rely on themselves to get what they want.

Cynicism is contagious, so mentioning cynical thoughts, even in passing, often rubs off on other people. Consider your evolution of friendships over the years. Have you stayed with the same group of friends, or have you moved on to a different style? Most people change their opinions over time, and a large part of that has to do with the people with which they spend time. If you are constantly exposed to an opinion, you will likely become resolved in its defense.

Cynicism grows in the constant critique of yourself and others. Critique, though helpful in growth, can overpower critical thinking by cementing thought patterns into your mind that are difficult to replace. You begin to think the worst in humanity, deepening your resentment.

Critical thinkers only use cynicism if it is warranted. That means that they only use cynicism after all other options are exhausted. The only way to solve problems is to be assured that they are solvable, even if the way to get there is difficult.

However, cynicism is difficult to overcome, especially if you feel naturally drawn to it. To overcome it, you must surround yourself with people who are both positive and have a tendency to believe in difficult things. Just as it is comfortable to spend time with people who think and feel the way you do, it is common to grasp onto cynical thoughts when you are in the presence of cynical people.

The truly destructive part of cynicism is becoming so involved in your disbelief that you believe you cannot change. Suddenly, cynicism becomes an endless cycle from which you cannot escape. You become buried in your own thoughts, preventing you from thinking wisely.

Find a way of communicating with others that will give your ideas plausibility while not shutting down those around you. You must be willing to learn new things and admit that you were wrong. Cynics believe that their opinions are the only relevant opinions, stopping helpful communication. Learn to grow from what others see and accept new ideas.

Become humble. This is a large part of communication but deserves its own category. Pride is off-putting, so even if you get your point across, others are not likely to listen, and you certainly will not change. Those with pride lift themselves up and become an island of thought.

Become curious again. As children, it is easy to want to discover the world, but as an adult, it becomes more difficult. Find something that fascinates you and start to study. Inevitably, you will come across someone who knows more about the subject than you do, which opens your lines of communication. You can learn from those who agree with you, but you learn more from those who do not.

If you are interested in trying something out of the ordinary, attempt hypnosis. For some, this mind-opening technique is enough to set them on the right path of being willing to believe in new things again. There are several online sources that can help you overcome cynicism.

Skepticism

Many mistake cynicism for skepticism, but in reality, they are two different concepts. While cynics constantly reject ideas, skeptics typically reject things they cannot explain with science. Skeptics are more prone to believe something if a proper scientific method is applied. As such, things that many people believe are beyond understanding--like religion and the paranormal—are often subjected to ridicule. Skeptics have the motto, "I'll believe it when I see it."

Many believe that skeptics are atheists because they do not believe in the supernatural, but skepticism is something that everyone practices. If you did not, you would have strong beliefs. Skepticism innately compares itself with opposite views and thereby dictates the best beliefs.

In many cases, people assume that skeptics have a devout mission to prove everyone wrong, and that may be true sometimes. However, with a healthy amount of skepticism, you are willing to believe that there are instances of unproven circumstances.

When too skeptical about aspects of life, critical thinking is ultimately demolished. Consider a skeptic from several hundred years ago, living in an age where the only way to get around was with a horse and cart. If you went back in time and told her that you had the technology to get from one place to the other at speeds more than 5 times what it takes for her to get places, she would not believe you.

Because she was unwilling to believe that there was such a device without seeing it for herself, she closed her mind to the possibilities. In some cases, magic was just science unknown to someone else. So, if you refuse to believe in something that you cannot quantify, you are shutting down your brain to the possibilities of the future.

Critical thinkers allow the possibility of extraordinary conditions. For example, the $100,000 challenge asks for challengers to prove their supernatural abilities. If they can, they are awarded the prize money; if they cannot, they are no worse off, except perhaps a little more defeated. The challenge realizes the possibility of supernatural occurrences, but they want to see it for themselves.

Since skepticism is fundamentally different from cynicism, it is possible to be humble and curious while still being skeptical. However, if you find yourself becoming too skeptical, become a proponent for the truth and open yourself up to new ideas. Skepticism is the road to cynicism, so be aware of how you respond to other data.

Narrow-Mindedness

It is easy to be narrow-minded since there are so many ways to believe that you are right and someone else is wrong. Though narrow-mindedness is similar to skepticism and cynicism, it differs in one significant way: you refuse to accept differing opinions, even if they show proven correct.

One common example is social media. For many, social media breeds narrow-mindedness like cancer. Emotions are often involved in opinions, preventing others from thinking clearly. In many cases, some are so entrenched in their own ideas that they either do not see or understand facts.

Offense is often a sign of narrow-mindedness. Critical thinkers can look at two sides of an issue and determine where the facts point, but narrow-minded people take offense to things they cannot explain. The "safe zone" of many institutions, including social media, is a form of narrow-mindedness since difficult subjects cannot be raised for fear of offending someone.

Narrow-minded people are often highly judgmental. After all, how else would they be able to discern if something was offensive or not? These people are also highly involved in others' relationships. They believe that they know what is best for those around them, often negating the feelings of others.

Bad habits die hard, or at least the saying goes. For narrow-minded people, getting rid of old habits is difficult, mostly because they have been stuck in the same routine for many years. They may succumb to road rage, a habit they've had since they got their licenses, or they constantly complain about a job they have no intention of leaving. Narrow-minded people find it difficult to accept change of any kind, which may include new information.

The only way to open your mind is through practice. It may be that you refuse to get angry when a friend disagrees with you, or you may pass up the chance to comment on social media. Try to put yourself in someone else's shoes. When you do, you open your mind to critical thinking. You become more aware of other facts and opinions, often leading to a better understanding of issues.

Try new things. Often, trying something that someone else does is a great way to help you become more aware of ideas you previously hadn't. If you have racist tendencies, spend more time with people of other colors. If you have an aversion to spiritual or paranormal phenomenon, study one.

Rationalization and Doublethink

When was the last time you told yourself that someone else was wrong about something because you could not face up to the fact that you had made a wrong decision? Many people blame professors for bad grades, bosses for firings, or dogs for biting when they fail. When you do this, your mind becomes closed to the possibility of improvement.

Of course, rationalization is not something borne of ill feelings. In most cases, it is a defense mechanism aimed to help you recover from a failure. However, becoming too reliant on it causes problems. Soon, rationalization leads to closed-mindedness, since you are no longer willing to believe that you made a rash decision.

Doublethink is the tendency to think two contrary things at the same time, and it is common in addiction cases. Alcoholics have a tendency to think that they can stop drinking while at the same time knowing that they cannot. Addicts use the phrase "I can stop anytime," as a rationalization for their behavior, when they know they are in trouble.

Doublethink was first introduced in George Orwell's 1984. The dystopian novel's main character is subjected to an overpowering government called Big Brother. Big Brother sees and hears everything, even what they think. As a defense mechanism, the main character utilizes doublethink, which essentially allows him to believe his own lies. He has become so indoctrinated, that he cannot wrench himself away from the thoughts.

Non-addicts use this method, too. When was the last time you told yourself that tomatoes were healthy, so ketchup was, too? You know that the food is not healthy, but it is nearly impossible to pull yourself from it, unless you start thinking critically, which means giving up delusions.

Stress

Like fear, stress turns off your brain. Stress can have such a high impact on your brain that you may be reduced to the thoughts of a child, one study says. You can only imagine the effects of chronic stress, then, and its association with anxiety disorders. Long-term effects can affect the way you learn, make decisions, and remember.

Stress causes the brain to produce fewer neurons than when not experiencing stress. The hippocampus is negatively affected, causing difficulty in thinking critically. So, the long-term effects play a significant role. Even if you do not have an anxiety disorder now, it is possible to develop one later in life through chronic stress.

White matter, though less commonly known than gray matter, is important to the brain's function. White matter creates pathways in the brain that allows it to communicate with other parts. Prolonged stress creates an excess of white matter, which causes too many connections in the brain and literally rewires you. The earlier you experience chronic stress, the more likely you are to develop mental illnesses in the future.

Stress also causes the brain to shrink. Though this can happen at any age, it is prevalent among the young. Even temporary stress can cause brain shrinkage. Unfortunately, stresses build on each other, causing them to further the risks of mental illness and the loss of critical thinking.

It is obvious that stress plays a negative role in the body and the mind, which makes it difficult to function. However, some are more affected by stress than others. Those who have learned to adapt to stressful situations are more likely to think clearly later.

Chapter 5:

9 Actionable Strategies for Strengthening Logical Thought

It can seem overwhelming to see all of the ways that your brain can fool you into not using critical thinking skills. In many cases, the brain becomes so entrenched in what it has learned that it becomes increasingly difficult to change habits and moods. However, there are ways to strengthen your critical thinking skills in everyday life, and it may be easier than you think.

First, remember to not get discouraged if you do not progress as quickly as you would like. The brain needs time to rewire itself, and sometimes that means taking a break from critical thinking. Wherever you are in the process, there is always time to increase your skills at a rate at which you are comfortable. Consider these nine strategies to help you strengthen your logical thought.

1.   **Practice**

Questioning

Questioning sounds easy enough. In fact, one of the easiest parts of critical thinking is coming up with questions. However, it takes more than that to think critically. Avoid questions that are easily answered with a one-dimensional response. Sidestep questions to which you already know the answers. Questions such as, "Am I able to skip?" are irrelevant and only useful to stroke your ego, if that.

If you already know the answers to more difficult questions, attempt to delve deeper into understanding them. You may have learned why the sky is blue in grade school, but how much do you actually know about the refraction of light? To that end, how much do you know about the water molecules themselves? When you ask questions with open answers, you begin to use critical thinking skills.

Bloom's Taxonomy for Critical Thinking

Bloom's taxonomy gives a hierarchy of cognitive processes that breaks down how to ask questions that will challenge your thought process.

1. _Knowledge_:

Your knowledge is your ability to remember information. If you remember the year that began the French Revolution, you are recovering knowledge. This is the first step in thinking critically. When a politician argues that global warming will end the world in 12 years, your first response should be to remember information you have about the subject. You could cite arguments both agreeing and disagreeing with the claim.

Before you can question effectively, you must be able to have basic information about the subject. Begin to ask yourself 'what' questions: "What are the primary colors?" "What are the strengths and weaknesses of this argument?" "What is the most important equation to remember on an exam?"

Another basic knowledge question is 'who?' This question often results in very short answers, perfect for gaining knowledge: "Who will this benefit?" "Who am I going to affect if I choose this course of action?" "Who are the people responsible for this award?"

The beginning of critical thought is forming a basis for future questions. So, you may need to think critically about what basic information you need to gather about an issue. As soon as you have a topic, break it down into the knowledge you need to accomplish a task.

2. _Comprehension_:

The next step is being able to interpret the information. When studying for a math test, you may be tempted to memorize all of the practice test problems with the hope of getting a good grade, but you are hardly comprehending the information. Interpret information by putting things in your own words. You only truly know something when you can teach it to someone else.

Understanding a question means asking *how* something occurs. The beginning of comprehension starts with 'how' questions: "How does this affect me in the future?" "How do I know this proof is correct?" "How can I change this for the better?" "How" questions force the mind to think logically. Do not allow yourself to resort to the quick response, "It works because it does."

'Why' is another question related to comprehension. As soon as you know *how* something works, determine *why* it works. Again, falling into the trap of assuming you cannot find the answer stops critical thinking. If you are frustrated, ask simple 'why' questions to lead up to more complicated questioning: "Why does a car run on gasoline?" "Why has this tradition lasted so long?" "Why is this the best way to do things?"

Often, the comprehension stage makes you aware of how well you know a material, and that can be uncomfortable. However, open-mindedness requires you to go outside of your comfort zone.

   3. *Application*:

Physicists say that physics is simply applied math. Physicists ask questions for practically any subject and attempt to answer them mathematically. This application of knowledge is the next stage of understanding because it requires you to know the mechanics of your information.

"When" questions are at the heart of the application process. Though they may seem like knowledge questions, *when* requires you to know when to apply your findings. Some simple 'when' questions may include: "When should I use this mathematical equation to simplify this answer?" "When would this benefit the community?" "When has history repeated itself?"

"Where" questions are just as important as 'when' questions. They force you to take the information you have learned and integrate it into new theories or old knowledge. Some 'where' questions include: "Where can I put this mechanism into the electrical system to produce energy?" "Where can we improve this function?" "Where would I need this technology the most?"

The application step utilizes the information you have gathered and applies it where necessary. Since you already understand the mechanics, this step allows you to more easily resolve difficult questions.

How Questions are Used

Questions do not have to fall under the category, "because I want to know stuff." As soon as questions are answered, analyze what you have learned. Determine the internal links between the information you have learned and applied. Analyzation is the prime method for discovery. Everything must be checked twice to be verified.

Questions are often used to change beliefs and arguments. It is not uncommon to flip your viewpoint after learning the facts. That is what a good critical thinker should do.

2. Become Aware of Your Mental Process

When was the last time you wrote something down with pen and paper? If you are like most people, it has probably been some time. However, physically writing things down can help you become more aware of what you are writing, and you are more likely to remember it.

Everyone has a different learning style, and it is important to learn yours. When you understand how you learn, it becomes easier to process information. In general, there are six types of learners: visual, aural, print, tactile, interactive, and kinesthetic. Though everyone is a mixture of at least two of these types, you might discover that you are better able to understand your mental process.

Visual thinkers like to look at presentations, pictures, and even words. If you like to look at what is on the screen for a PowerPoint presentation instead of listening to the speaker, you like to think visually. Create an environment that makes it easy to learn this way. Draw pictures or diagrams to help you process information.

Aural learners prefer to hear what they learn. This may mean that you are more likely to enjoy lectures, or you may simply enjoy listening to audiobooks instead of reading. There are many books on tape that help develop skills, and you can listen to them as you do other tasks.

Print learners prefer to write things down. If you like to develop lists, you may be a print learner. Some print learners write notes and never look at them again. The process of writing helps them remember more than any other method. Studies have shown that everyone benefits from writing things down when it comes to remembering.

Tactile thinkers need to work with their hands. They prefer subjects like mechanics or ceramics, something they can understand while touching. Tactile learners also tend to have a harder time understanding things that are not tangible, like mathematics. This does not mean that you cannot learn to think critically as a tactile learner.

Interactive learners like to discuss what they think. Have you ever been in a room with someone who is determined to talk to anyone and everyone who is involved in a project? They thrive in conversation.

Kinesthetic learners prefer movement in learning. If moving around, even walking as learning, you are a kinesthetic learner. These people prefer roleplay to sitting in a lecture, and interactive lessons are the best. Create a movement with your thought process, perhaps working with others to develop ideas and acting them out.

You can also learn more about your mental process by discovering your biases. Be aware of how you respond to others. In many cases, your biases manifest themselves through emotion. Do not take shortcuts, and develop techniques to strengthen your weaknesses in thought.

3. Socializing

Think of the last time you spent time with someone with a different point of view. It may have been a professor, or it could have been a friend of a friend. If they taught you something new, you used your critical thinking skills. Though it is always helpful to get a fresh perspective from a friend, they often have many of the same opinions as you, which makes conversation easy. However, if you join a group with more differences than you, you will start to develop better thought processes.

Critical thinking is not easy, and it should not be. It should test your boundaries. It may be difficult to hear differing opinions without expressing emotion, but once you get the hang of it, it becomes vastly more meaningful than hearing the same opinions rehashed. Remember, it is important to surround yourself with people who have different cognitive biases. Lazy thinking is contagious, so do not fall into the same trap.

Develop relationships that last. Find a mentor that is open to answering questions, and create a sense of humility. Socializing makes asking questions easier. While otherwise you might have to wade through sources that may or may not be correct, asking questions to someone knowledgeable in an area different than yours can give you insights you might not have seen otherwise.

4.   Do   Logical
Thinking Exercises

Because critical thinking is often associated with work, many find it difficult to get the motivation to practice. However, there are exercises that work your brain and offer a fun escape from daily life.

1. _Puzzles_:

Brain teasers and puzzles are some of the most common forms of critical thinking exercises. If you have time, open a local paper and work a Sudoku puzzle. Many cell phones offer apps that can be a great distraction. Use riddles to test your knowledge of language and reasoning. Consider the example below:

A house set on a hill has windows on all sides.

Every window faces south.

A bear walks by; what color is the bear?

If you answered *white*, you are correct. If not, use the answer to logically come to a conclusion. Try this next example found in J.R.R. Tolkien's *The Hobbit*:

This thing all things devours:

Birds, beasts, trees, flowers;

Gnaws iron, bites steel;

Grinds hard stones to meal;

Slays king, ruins town,

And beats high mountain down.

This classic riddle's answer is *time*. If you have not read the book, use your time to increase your critical thinking abilities and read it.

2. *Read*:

Speaking of reading, one of the best ways to increase your brain capacity is to delve into a good book. If you love mysteries, delve into books such as *The Woman in White* written by Wilkie Collins or *Murder on the Orient Express* by Agatha Cristie. Try to solve the puzzles as you read.

While there are thousands of entertaining books in the world, you will get the most out of reading subjects that challenge you. Some of these books are philosophical, such as C.S. Lewis's *The Weight of Glory*, or books that delve into difficult subjects, such as *Fahrenheit 451* by Ray Bradbury. Some of the books that help critical thinking the most do not come in novel-form. Challenge yourself by pushing your boundaries.

3. *Mathematical Problems*:

You may be among the many if you groaned as you read this in the list. Mathematical problems can seem boring, especially if you do not understand the concepts. However, if you spend time gaining mathematical understanding, you may find yourself enjoying the problems. Consider Einstein's mathematical problem and see if you can get the answer.

Eight married couples meet to lend one another some books. Couples have the same surname, employment and car. Each couple has a favorite color. Furthermore we know the following facts:

1. Daniella Black and her husband work as Shop-Assistants.

2. The book "The Seadog" was brought by a couple who drive a Fiat and love the color red.

3. Owen and his wife Victoria like the color brown.

4. Stan Horricks and his wife Hannah like the color white.

5. Jenny Smith and her husband work as Warehouse Managers and they drive a Wartburg.

6. Monica and her husband Alexander borrowed the book "Grandfather Joseph."

7. Mathew and his wife like the color pink and brought the book "Mulatka Gabriela."

8. Irene and her husband Oto work as Accountants.

9. The book "We Were Five" was borrowed by a couple driving a Trabant.

10. The Cermaks are both Ticket-Collectors who brought the book "Shed Stoat."

11. Mr. and Mrs. Kuril are both Doctors who borrowed the book "Slovacko Judge."

12. Paul and his wife like the color green.

13. Veronica Dvorak and her husband like the color blue.

14. Rick and his wife brought the book "Slovacko Judge" and they drive a Ziguli.

15. One couple brought the book "Dame Commissar" and borrowed the book "Mulatka Gabriela."

16. The couple who drive a Dacia, love the color violet.

17. The couple who work as Teachers borrowed the book "Dame Commissar."

18. The couple who work as Agriculturalists drive a Moskvic.

19. Pamela and her husband drive a Renault and brought the book "Grandfather Joseph."

20. Pamela and her husband borrowed the book that Mr. and Mrs. Zajac brought.

21. Robert and his wife like the color yellow and borrowed the book "The Modern Comedy."

22. Mr. and Mrs. Swain work as Shoppers.

23. "The Modern Comedy" was brought by a couple driving a Skoda.

Who likes Violet (Mathisfun, n.d.)?

Take some time before coming up with an answer. The answer is Monica and Alexander, but try it to see if you find a different one.

4. *Games*:

Games are great at forcing you to socialize and strategize. Some of the best games have a mixture of both. If you are looking for an icebreaker to get to know new people, suggest a game.

Ticket to Ride and *Risk* are two popular games that force you to think strategically. Both of these games also display geography, adding more knowledge to your repertoire. The game *Chronology* makes you create a timeline of events, giving you knowledge in history. The more cards you can place in the correct time frame, the closer you are to winning.

5.   Participate   in

Debates

Some people are born to debate. If you love to get into disagreements with your friends, this is the sport for you. However, the key to a good debate is letting both sides argue their points. This means that both sides must give the other time to give reasons for their points. Analyze each point, and if you are feeling up to the challenge, debate a side on which you disagree.

6.   Learn   a   New
Skill

Sometimes learning new skills is not linked directly to critical thinking, but it does allow you to think differently. For example, if you spend all of your time on the computer generating images for engineering, consider taking up knitting. This hobby forces you to use your hands in unusual ways. Anyone who practices becomes better over time.

New skills can also translate to other aspects of your life. For example, studying literature can develop your communication skills. Learning the piano can help you understand patterns in mathematics. Building furniture can develop your accuracy with drawing. Learning a new language develops your ability to plan since you must build vocabulary then create logical sentences.

Now that you have discovered which learning style you prefer, study another one. For example, many tactile learners assume they are not good at mathematics, so they do not try. However, developing a learning skill that is new can rewire your brain and force you to think outside the box.

Use your new learning skills to do assignments and will help you internalize new information. For example, if you are a tactile learner, you may find that visualizing your projects may not only help you learn better visually, but tactically.

7. Think in Reverse

Consider a mathematical problem. Many teachers encourage their students to work the problem backward after finishing it to better understand how they came to that conclusion. The steps in reverse offer not only a review of mathematical properties, but let you see how the problems make sense logically.

Now, consider creating a business plan to create an irrigation system that will solve their crop-growing crisis. The town is located near a cyanide deposit, making it difficult for plants to grow. They need to navigate water from a nearby spring to overcome the effects of the poison. Irrigation has failed in the past since water has seeped into the ground, contaminating it with high concentrations of cyanide near the spring.

The first step is to identify the problem and ask either how the problem is caused or what you can do to change it. The problem is cyanide in the water and the lack of proper irrigation. You will make matters worse by creating canals in the system by tilling the ground. You will also see negative effects by creating a pathway directly to the soil with cyanide. Already, the results show that direct irrigation into the soil will cause more cyanide contamination.

The reverse brainstorming has revealed a few important results: the water must not touch the contaminated soil and the direction of the pipeline must backtrack to settle in more favorable ground. From here, you can determine how best to create an irrigation system that will support your conclusions.

Not only will thinking in reverse help you solidify your understanding of tough materials, but it may also help you develop ideas quicker. Reverse brainstorming involves using the conclusion to find an alternative. You will realize what will make the situation worse, using critical thinking skills to prevent future problems. When you are stuck try reverse brainstorming to find the best results.

8. Do Not Assume You Are Right

One of the most damaging blows to critical thinking is being unwilling to admit that you might be wrong. You must be willing to take the fall to think critically. This is an automatic process, so it is difficult to overcome, but practice admitting you were wrong is the first step to overcome it. Develop logical thought before resorting to assumptions.

9. Work on Your Focus and Concentration

It is easier to say you will focus and concentrate than it is to do. However, there are ways you can increase your focus and concentration without driving yourself insane. The key is to take small steps. Athletes must start at the bottom and work their ways up to the top of their sports through constant strengthening, and your focus can improve your critical thinking in much the same way. Here are some ways you can learn to concentrate better.

1. *Create a List for Distractions*:

Since the internet has become such a large part of everyday life, it is easy to get distracted. From wondering what others think of your posts to wondering what the weather will be like tomorrow, there is no shortage of distractions. It may surprise you to know that, as soon as you become distracted, it can take up to 25 minutes to return to focus. If you are distracted often, you will waste most of your day.

To overcome this, create a list of your distractions and reference them when you feel your mind start to wander. Often, if you realize that you are distracted, you can return to focus. Every time a new distraction pops up, write it down on a paper and continue working.

2. *Build Willpower*:

Have you ever stared over at the cupboards of your apartment, longing for a cookie you know you should not have? At long last, you might justify eating just one, which leads to the entire box. Just as you need willpower to stick to a diet, so you need willpower to stick to your critical thinking goals. Build it up daily by rewarding yourself for extended periods of focus.

3. *Meditate*:

Meditation clears the mind of all distractions and allows you to focus on yourself. While you meditate, you build your mental muscles, letting you focus for longer periods of time. A study conducted on 140 students over an eight-week program showed that students who meditated daily showed a significant increase in concentration (McKay & McKay, 2020). Even short periods of meditation improve your overall focus.

Many have developed techniques for every occasion, but if you are just starting, simply focus on controlling your breath. Remove all stressors from your brain and let your body relax as you learn to focus.

4. *Exercise*:

In almost every blog page devoted to improving critical thinking, exercise is on the list. Exercise creates endorphins in the brain, which make you feel good and help you overcome distractions and stressors. These endorphins also help those suffering from mental illnesses overcome mental bogs. That is why experts suggest going for a walk if you are depressed.

Even if you hate to exercise, there are low-impact options that give you the same boosts without making you feel like you are going to die. Going for a walk in the sunshine, cleaning dishes, or simply getting up to stretch every once in a while improves concentration and makes you feel better.

5. *Listen Actively*:

It can be difficult to pay attention to what others have to say, especially if you are not interested in the subject. However, active listening can help you focus. Nod your head and interject with encouraging words. Really become a part of what the other person has to say, and you will find yourself growing more interested.

Chapter 6:

Exercising Logical

Thought in Everyday Life

Now that you have practiced some of these methods, it is time to start using them in everyday life. There are thousands of opportunities every week to start up intelligent conversations to help yourself and others grow. When you are on your own, you can practice critical thinking by being open to new thoughts.

Questions and Social Media

Fake news is becoming increasingly popular. Just look at the different news platforms and compare what they report. It is difficult to find any news source that is completely honest. So, it is increasingly important to use critical thinking skills to determine what is true and what is easy to believe.

Fake news is certainly easy to believe. Writers propagate falsehoods with the same vigor that real news does.

One of the most common types of fake news is deliberate misinformation. Writers use emotionally-charged language to hook readers and force them to read their articles. The goal is to make news easily believable so that readers will not try to verify the sources.

People who spread fake news also use clickbait as a way to draw in readers. They use shocking or incomplete titles to draw the reader in. They use titles such as "When I sat down at my computer, I couldn't believe it when…" and ultimately leave you hanging. Writers use this technique to drive traffic, which ultimately leads to an article with little to no value.

Social media is known for its high volume of shares, retweets, and reblogs. However, many times news articles simply become popularity contests with users challenging others by citing evidence that has not been verified. Emotions become so charged that proof becomes irrelevant.

However, if you are willing to think critically, there are several ways to spot these instances of fake news before you become emotionally invested. You will be helping your friends by not sharing incorrect information.

1. *Media Literacy*:

When learning to read, you learned individual letters before moving to words, to sentences, to paragraphs, then to full articles. Media literacy involves the same techniques to understand the various types of messages sent on social media. Media literacy allows you to dissect seller messages to get to the heart of what they want from you.

First, determine what their purpose is. Are they trying to sell you something, or do they want to spread misinformation for political purposes? Most of the time, fake news outlets push an agenda in their writing. If you feel swayed one way or another, the author is probably trying to elicit emotions, instigating fake news.

Next, identify keywords that trigger emotional responses. Charged words such as 'cheat,' 'fake,' or 'idiotic' are commonly used to force people to become invested in lies. If you were afraid of swallowing eight spiders each year while you slept, you were more likely to pass on that fake information. Learn how to read articles to separate fact from emotion.

2. _Who Created This?_

You can know how reliable a source of news is by who created it. In many cases, organizations trying to push causes, even though giving some correct information, twist the truth to sway you one way or another. Ask the following questions when checking the source: Are you aware of the author's expertise in his or her field? Does the organization offer free information about its site? Does the URL have a tilde in it (this is usually an indicator of a personal website)?

Search the internet to make sure it is a reputable site. Many major organizations have foundations in

LinkedIn, or other professional sites, giving evidence of its reputability. Note the suffix of the site. Most reputable sites have endings like .gov, .edu. or .org. Search the web to find other articles the author has written to prove they are offering good news.

3. *What is the Message?*

If you can only find the same information about the article on that site, there is a good chance that it is fake news. Reputable sources offer sources and links that prove they are getting the best information. The best sites also keep up to date on their information. Do not accept news that is several months old, and even a difference of weeks can prove an article incorrect. Ask yourself the following questions: Are there quotations from other sources? Is there a tone in the article that suggests it could be factual or opinion? Which side of the argument is being left out?

4. *Why Was This Created?*

If you have no idea why anyone would go to that site, there is a good chance that it is fake news. Opinion articles usually come with a stipulation: either you believe me or you are an idiot. If you get the feeling that the content was created only for the purpose of proving a point, you have the wrong site. Ask yourself the following questions: What was the motivation for the article? Is this an advertisement? Is this sponsored? If it is the latter, the author is getting paid to show these articles, hardly a foundation for a reasonable argument.

5. *Break it Down*:

After you have asked the questions about fake news, add critical thinking to the mix. Some reputable sources still provide fake news, and it is up to you to determine if all sides are considered. Be aware of what you usually fall for, and pay special attention to overcoming your personal obstacles.

Logical Debates With Friends

Take a good look at your friends. What do they believe? Again, charged words and phrases can bring out emotions, preventing real logical thought. However, if you analyze the kind of friends you keep, you can have logical debates without angering your group of friends.

It is easy to believe that your friends have your values at heart, but you may feel that way because they share the same values as you. Get the rest of your friend group actively thinking by questioning what you believe, but do so with tact. Often, presenting information in an approachable way benefits the whole group, you included. You should not have to lose friendships due to disagreements over points of logic.

Add new people to your friend group. People from other cultures offer fresh perspectives on life and social issues. Develop your discussions in a debate format and avoid screaming matches. If raised voices are inevitable, take a moment to remind everyone of your love for each other. None of you can think critically if you are all involved in a battle for dominance.

Make Logical Purchase Decisions

When was the last time you went to the grocery store nearly starved? You likely started munching on the food you picked up before you made it to the checkout line, and the best kind of food to munch on is easily-accessible food, which is usually bad for you. By the time you make it to the checkout line, your cart is full of products you do not need, and some you did not know you had grabbed.

You can learn to make logical purchase decisions by thinking clearly before you head into a store. Marketing ploys such as bright colors and moving objects often catch attention and make you want to purchase things you do not need. Advertisers cleverly put the items for sale at the front of the store, forcing you to walk all the way to the front to purchase them, often getting other items along the way.

To prevent a huge dent in your bank account, start to analyze what makes you susceptible to common ads. Can you not resist a sale? Do you love to buy things that fashion forward? Do you fall for the candy wrappers with delicious-looking food on the wrapper? The next time you are out shopping (in a store or online), keep a list of the things that affect you the most. As soon as you recognize them, they do not have as great a hold on you.

Evaluate your month's purchases. Are you susceptible to impulse buys, or do you find yourself sticking to a list? Writing down your budget and spending helps you think critically about the money you spend. Money becomes more difficult to spend when you realize how many bills you have to pay.

When buying, ask the right questions. Is your purchase something you really need? Are you spending money on things that are affected by other aspects of your life, like depression? Are you aware of the overpriced nature of items before buying them? Do you sift between different options? Develop a strategy to keep yourself on track.

Strengthen Communication

Communication is one of the most essential parts of any relationship. If a family is having financial trouble, it is because they are failing to communicate their wants and needs, ultimately resolving the issue. If a wife is unhappy with her husband, bottling up the emotions is what causes major fights later.

The secret to good communication is analyzing a situation and creating an avenue for the release of tension. In many cases, this includes understanding how another person behaves in stressful and bountiful situations. Slight changes in attitudes or emotions can be a tell-tale sign of improper communication.

Ask the right questions when communicating. How does my attitude affect the people around me? How can I influence someone else's life for the good through developing a strategy to effectively communicate my feelings? How can I develop a strategy for continued communication?

However, it is easy to get caught in the trap of believing that you know everything the other party thinks. The "you just don't get it, do you?" response to improper speculation often makes you wish you had reached for a Point-Of-View gun. Even if you have known someone for a long period of time, it is still possible to guess wrong when communicating. Before you make up your mind, listen to all sides. Make sure you put knowledge as the priority in any discussion.

Distance Yourself from Feelings

As mentioned previously, it is impossible to completely separate yourself from emotions, but you must keep an open mind when communicating with others. An open mind usually means the stabilization of emotions. Consider arguing with a friend about something you really care about. It was nearly impossible to feel that they are not personally attacking you when they attack your beliefs.

To distance yourself from emotions, come to know what triggers you, what makes you fly off the handle, and what makes you satisfied. The first step to understanding others is understanding yourself. Recognize yourself when you get offended. Again, being closed-minded is detrimental to critical thinking, and your emotions can get in the way.

When you feel yourself losing control of a conversation, it is only natural to feel overwhelmed and angry, which arises from fear. Remember that you do not need to be in control of a conversation, only of your own critical thinking skills. Once you adopt this attitude, you will regain control. You will also be able to better control your anger and frustrations.

Remember to have a healthy distance from feelings. If you start to feel isolated, depressed, or anxious, curb your detachment. Leaning too far in this direction is just as damaging as becoming too emotional. However, once you understand your emotions better, you can detach more effectively and with little damage.

Positive emotions, such as joy and euphoria, can also cloud your judgment. You may become so enthralled in your emotions that you forget that they do not allow you to feel skeptical about new beliefs. You will start to overestimate the prospects for success, thereby hindering critical thought.

Develop the most effective ways for you to separate your emotions by learning how to cool off effectively. Here are some ways to do so:

1. *Take a Break*:

Sometimes the best thing you can do for yourself and others is to take a break from your thoughts and instead focus on getting your emotions under control. This may include taking a break from people in general. It is easy to feel victimized if you are constantly on the defensive when trying to analyze all areas of a discussion.

Feeling overwhelmed often requires a break from the world to gather thoughts. Do not drift into stressful situations if you can help it. Allow yourself to heal after difficult discussions with charged emotions.

2. *Sleep on It*:

One of the most popular pieces of advice for married couples is to not go to bed angry, but sometimes it is the best solution. A lack of sleep lowers your capability for thinking logically, which often results in explosive emotions. When you are tired, it is easier to feel fear since you are in a vulnerable situation. This is a result of years of hunter and gatherer ancestry. If you were tired, you were at risk from predators, so early humans were more prone to have a heightened sense of fear to keep them alert.

It is also difficult to think critically when tired. Just like with its response to fear, the body allocates the blood to parts of the body that may need it in a fight-or-flight situation.

3. *Start Journaling*:

Sometimes when you have a million thoughts in your head, it is difficult to separate the logical thoughts from the emotional ones. Journaling allows you to get emotions out of your brain and focus on thinking critically. Journaling is a form of meditation, which also focuses the mind.

Apply, Apply, Apply

Once you have learned how to improve your critical thinking skills, use your newly-found superpower to help you overcome obstacles and develop a sense of understanding of others and the world around you. You can use these principles in your everyday life, and they are extremely important to relationships and careers, so keep practicing.

Chapter 7:

Language, Thought, and

Logic

Language plays an integral part in logic. The combinations of sounds and repetition is closely related to critical thinking. The variation of language is extremely complex, yet our minds can still process slight changes in sounds we hear. We are able to break down the sounds heard into numbers, people, places, and things based on a mutual agreement from other people.

When you consider the complexities of language, everyone is a critical thinker. They are able to comprehend a complex system of arbitrary letters and numbers that dictate how we communicate with one another. The meanings of words are determined by a consensus that has nothing to do with the letters that are put together. Language, therefore, is a mutual agreement of memorized words that control human thought and emotion.

Those who have learned more than one language know that, after learning one language, learning another is not difficult. Perhaps the reason for this lies in the way language is related to mathematics. The brain is able to comprehend complex patterns and relate them to the order of sounds.

Language and Mathematics

Language ultimately affects the way we think, even processing the way we conceptualize numbers. Studies conducted in tribes of the Amazon tested how well deaf people were able to conceptualize a number of objects based on the numbers used in their counting systems. These tribes required a sign for the numbers in the system to easily conceptualize what they saw.

The deaf members of the tribes had a limited number of signs for numbers. In one case, one tribe could only count by one, two, many, and any number beyond the number two became difficult to comprehend. The tribes that had a larger vocabulary for numbered words were able to better answer the questions.

Researchers tested the comprehension of students in Nicaragua. Though there was a school developed in 1970, there were many students who used "home signs" as developed words, but these signs lacked the patterned behavior of normal language and had few signs for numbered words. Their phrases were disjointed and they only understood the signs for words they had created. Over the course of several years in the late 2000s, researchers compared how well these "home signers" could comprehend numbers compared to the students who went to the deaf school in Nicaragua.

First, researchers gave a story about frogs and lilypads. There were originally eight frogs, but four jumped away, and two came back. They were asked to recount this story to a friend to determine comprehension. Remarkably, these home signers had difficulties explaining the number of frogs after the number surpassed two. Even though they used their fingers to indicate how many frogs were in the pond, the comprehension plummeted with no words to explain the numbers.

Elizabeth Spaepen, a researcher in the group, noted that these home signers could not understand the concept of a number like the seven. They only understood one-one-one-one-one-one-one (Grossman, 2011). This kind of concept is reminiscent of how children count. In many cases, they use their fingers to understand the concept of multiple numbers, but it takes years for them to develop an understanding of larger numbers.

Areas Responsible for Logical Thought

There are specific parts of language that affect the way we think. The connections we make in the brain are dictated by how we understand language. Concepts such as word choice, vocabulary definitions, and interpretations play a large role in understanding critical thought.

Word Choice

Consider a story with a standard vocabulary: When I was young, I used to think that there was popcorn growing on apricot trees instead of blossoms. When I asked my mother if I could go out and pick the popcorn from the trees, she looked surprised, and it was only after I showed her the popcorn on the trees that she finally understood and laughed.

Now, let us change this basic story by altering some of the words in it: When I was young, I insisted that there was popcorn sprouting from the apricot trees instead of blossoms. When I pleaded with my mother to go out and scoop up the popcorn growing from the trees, she looked frightened, and it was only after I forced her to gaze upon the trees that she looked relieved and laughed.

These two stories are relatively the same, though the word choice in the second example changes the meaning from an innocent mistake to a mother's fear for her child's sanity. Though the words hold relatively the same meanings, the differences lie in the connotations. Replacing the word 'thought' with 'insisted' gives the new story a sense of desperation. The two interpretations of the stories can give drastically different responses in the brain. It is ultimately word choice that determines the meaning.

Word choice also affects inner dialogue. Whether you are eternally optimistic or would rather see the glass as half empty, the way you use words changes their meanings in your head. Your inner dialogue is how you interpret the world. Since the brain is ultimately connected through its perceptions of the world and inner dialogue, you can change any thought to be positive or negative.

Studies have shown that words as simple as 'yes' and 'no' have a profound influence on how you react to life. Where the word 'yes' can make you feel elated, the word 'no' can feel like a punch in the gut in the wrong circumstances.

Researchers attempted to simulate the effects that word choice can have on the brain. They first created visual noise by showing the image of a chair to one eye and showing squiggling lines to the other eye. Due to the visual noise, participants were not able to determine what the image was. However, when researchers told the participants that they were viewing a chair, the visual noise was wiped out.

Language plays a part in sensory perception as well. You can alter the way you perceive pain by altering your internal dialogue. If you believe that you cannot feel pain, you will not experience it. This also means that you can change the way you discern touch. Your mind can influence you into believing that you are being touched, just by hearing a suggestion.

Vocabulary Definitions and Ambiguity

Ambiguity affects the way that words are perceived. Famous writers have used this tool for readers to interpret their words in ways different to every person. View this example from Shakespeare to examine ambiguity.

> *When my love swears that she is made of truth,*
> *I do believe her, though I know she lies,*
> *That she might think me some untutored youth,*
> *Unlearnèd in the world's false subtleties.*
> *Thus vainly thinking that she thinks me young,*
> *Although she knows my days are past the best,*
> *Simply I credit her false-speaking tongue:*
> *On both sides thus is simple truth suppressed.*
> *But wherefore says she not she is unjust?*
> *And wherefore say not I that I am old?*
> *Oh, love's best habit is in seeming trust,*
> *And age in love loves not to have years told.*
> *Therefore I lie with her and she with me,*
> *And in our faults by lies we flattered be (Sonnet 138).*

He flirts with claiming deception from the woman while not explicitly saying so. Use your critical thinking skills to determine more ambiguous language. What can you see here beyond the surface?

Since English is such a melting pot of a language, it includes many words that mean the same thing, but have different connotations. How, then, can you know exactly what something means? Critical thinking involves breaking sentences down to better understand what they mean.

The way you interpret words varies greatly from another with a different background. Think, for example, of what you think of when you imagine a garden. To you, it may mean hard work and long hours, while to someone else it may mean the epitome of class and breeding. The way you define words, in turn, defines you.

Interpretation

Interpretation does not only mean translating languages; it also means interpreting emotions and connotations. For example, the word 'nosy' has a negative connotation, while the word 'interested,' essentially meaning the same thing, denotes a positive connotation.

Imagine how much easier it is to communicate with others by using language that is associated with positive connotations. When you describe someone's tenacity, you could either explain it as 'steadfastness' or 'stubbornness.' This emotionally charged second option will likely close minds and prevent you from properly advocating for your role to increase knowledge.

Be aware of abusive and demeaning language not only in others, but also in yourself. If you have been in the habit of saying socially unacceptable things, try interpreting your words to allow for greater critical thinking. People use this type of language to shock others into forming opinions quickly, which is never a healthy way to initiate critical thinking.

How to Be a Better Logical Thinker

The best way to be a logical thinker is to invest in yourself. You have everything you need to succeed, all it takes is practice and application. However, it is always important to expand your horizons. What may seem profoundly boring to you may become your favorite subject after multiple hours of appreciation for its nuances. If you want to become a better critical thinker, put in the effort.

Read More

Successful people read more. Why? Because they see what others have done and attempt to either emulate or outshine them. Critical thinkers know how to break down literature into lessons and altering viewpoints. Readers are also more open to new ideas. Many authors do not have the same sets of values as their readers, but they can relay information in a way that is easy to understand.

Language is such an important part of critical thinking because it allows the reader to examine different points of view and change the way they interpret information forever. Connections grow in the brain by practicing good reading skills and thinking critically while expanding horizons.

Read in a variety of different subjects. The more you read, the more you learn, and only sticking with books about pirates, though interesting, will not expand your worldview. The only way to grow is to learn something different. Differing points of view are vital to think critically. Many books either glorify or denounce war, and though you may agree with one view over the other, it is important to think about why this is. You may begin to understand why people fight in the first place.

Put your knowledge to test and read things that challenge what you know. Many people become stuck in believing that they have the most recent information, when there is a wealth of added knowledge that will help you grow. If you are unsure about the legitimacy of the information you read, exercise your skills of deduction to determine the correct answers and find sources that back up your claims.

Enrich Language

When was the last time you learned a new word? If you have spent most of your time looking at news on social media, it is likely that you have not learned something new for a long time. The process of gaining knowledge about language helps you to better communicate and interpret information.

Bloom's taxonomy defined the process of cognitive thought, and enriching your language not only builds your knowledge base, but helps you analyze and interpret new information as it comes along. The effort you put into developing an understanding of language translates to logically thinking.

If you get the opportunity, learn another language. They say that, after you learn a second language, others come easier. This is because of the patterns in language. Because direct translations often do not make complete sense, interpretation, forces you to examine grammar and syntax. Your mind will become accustomed to translating language, forcing your mind to work in overdrive and enhancing logical thinking.

Soft Skills

Soft skills such as communication and emotional intelligence are often on the backburner for people who believe that critical thinking only involves breaking down puzzles. However, as you have learned from previous chapters, there is much more to critical thinking than plugging numbers into an equation.

Practice adapting to different situations. Adaptation skills allow you to process information faster and with more accuracy. You will not become bogged down by emotions when attempting to debate. Instead, adaptation lets you address every situation as it arises.

Grow your leadership skills by directing thought for yourself and others. In many cases, this could include mediating debates or setting a tone for an argument. When you are in a meeting, develop ways to connect with those around you to better communicate information.

Articulation

Do not fall into the trap of ambiguity unless you are trying to instill thoughts in others. Many who attempt ambiguous language do not actually know what they are talking about and only apply generalizations in an attempt to sound clever. Analyze your words and phrases before communicating with others.

If you are not careful with your language, you can cause closed-mindedness in others, preventing you from reaching them. Use language that is not emotionally charged, and develop your own vocabulary to better send messages.

Becoming a Critical Thinker

Critical thinking takes time and practice, but it does not have to be boring. In fact, the more fun you make it, the greater chance it will stick with you. Develop your own sense of understanding of both yourself and others. Study psychology to determine how others react, and attempt to find these reactions in yourself. You may find that interacting with others becomes easier after a while.

You are in charge of your own destiny, which means that you are responsible for making your life a better one. The only way to become a critical thinker is to start, which means you must be willing to participate in events out of your comfort zone. Encourage others to follow in your footsteps, and soon you will be surrounded by people eager to engage in logical thinking exercises.

Conclusion

Many people struggle to get their bearings when learning how to think critically. It is not something that comes naturally to everyone. However, it is something that all humans are able to achieve due to increased learning. From the dawn of time until now, humans have developed ways to strategize, ways to think, and ways to interpret feelings and knowledge.

This book was created to build your skills when it comes to logical thinking. That means that you will be able to increase your capacity for learning by following the steps outlined here. The most important part of it is taking the information and applying it to your life.

Logical thinking is the process by which you learn to reason given information and your ability to interpret data. In essence, it is eliminating any false notions to guide your way to objective truth. Left and right hemispheres of the brain have long been speculated to be separated, the left designated for logical thinking while the right is in charge of creativity. However, recent studies have determined that there is a deep connection to the two, and no one can live simply as a left or right brained person.

The gray matter in the brain is connected with white matter, which sends information from each section of the brain. Though there are two distinctive hemispheres, they are in constant contact with each other. The right side of the brain usually gives broader understanding while the left side of the brain is focused. It is important to let your right side of the brain be free while making the left side an obedient servant. Though there are many theories about the workings of the brain, it has thus far been impossible to accurately navigate the brain.

Aristotle broke down logic into three laws: the law of noncontradiction, the law of excluded middle, and the principle of identity. The law of noncontradiction states that two opposing views cannot equal the same thing. The law of excluded middle states that there is no middle ground between right and wrong; the two are polar opposites. Finally, the principle of identity states that anything must equal itself.

Logical thinking requires the use of these three laws for inductive and deductive reasoning. Both of these methods search for objective truth, but they are conducted in opposite directions. The results of a logical exercise are either sound or unsound, based on the logic of the arguments. Premises must be true and valid to pass the test of a successful argument. The critical thinking process is broken down into the following steps: gather information, analyze information, question, identify your assumptions and biases, put the information in context, and reach a conclusion.

Cognitive bias is often the reason for flawed thinking. Confirmation bias instills your own beliefs by surrounding yourself with people who think the same as you. Anchoring bias unconsciously ties you to the first piece of information you learn. Hindsight bias makes you claim that you knew it all along. The misinformation effect demonstrates how easily memories can be manipulated. The actor observer bias forces you to attribute your problems to some outside stimulus. The false consensus bias makes you believe that how you act and think is common. The halo effect influences the way you perceive others by your initial impressions of them. The self-serving bias is a behavioral defense that associates the good with themselves and the bad with external interactions. The availability heuristic is a mental shortcut that allows you to process information faster, but not always accurately. The optimism bias makes you always hope for the best.

Emotions and intuition play a large part in how we interpret bias and utilize it in daily life. Anger, fear, and happiness ultimately affect the way we process information. There is no disposition to thinking critically, which is why it is vitally important to practice, so it becomes second nature.

We tend to think illogically because of our inner beliefs. Cynicism causes the mind to reject any new information, even if it has been proven correct. Cynics are unwilling to change their behaviors to better suit learning. Skeptics are a slightly less extreme version of cynics, requiring proof before they believe anything definitively. Both of these thought processes are prone to closed-mindedness. It takes practice to open up about new information and accept change.

We often rationalize and use doublethink to justify our actions. These practices prevent the mind from fully accepting new information. People who doublethink say something enough to the point that they believe it themselves, which is damaging to the understanding of critical thought. Stress negatively affects the mind as well, often returning the brain to an adolescent stage since blood does not flow freely to the brain.

Become a master strategizer by strengthening your logical thoughts by practicing asking questions. The cognitive thought process is based on the foundation of questions, and asking the most basic questions allows the mind to open. Become more aware of your mental process. That means taking notes frequently and noting how you can improve. Socialize with a wide range of people to broaden your horizons and improve your critical thought. Practice puzzles, games, riddles, and toys to get practice. Develop your reasoning for solving puzzles and develop your own riddles. Take part in debates with friends to simulate listening to both sides of an argument. Learn a new skill and use your learning capabilities as a basis for understanding how to increase your logical thought in the future. Try reverse brainstorming and work on your focus and concentration. Finally, do not always assume you are right. Give yourself the option to be wrong.

You can exercise your logical muscles by asking questions, the right questions. Discover where you stand in social media, and make educated conclusions based on what you find. Spark debates with friends, but do not fall into the trap of becoming emotional while you do so. When you learn a new skill, you are able to use different parts of your brain to understand how others think and how to interpret information. Use critical thinking to make logical purchase choices, and study advertisements to better understand how you are influenced. Strengthen communication by developing skills to help you better understand others. Though it is impossible to completely remove your emotions, create a logical distance so you can understand why you feel the way you do.

Language is the basis for logical thought since it is so uniquely connected with the way we communicate with ourselves and others. Be aware of your word and phrase choices to make the most logical conclusions. Define vocabulary, and avoid arbitrary language. Learn to interpret emotions and words to better communicate.

Ultimately, the best way to become a logical thinker is to practice using literature. Read more and use a wide variety of subjects. Enrich your language by studying new words and interpreting the way language behaves. Use your soft skills to enhance your problem-solving abilities. Finally, focus on articulation to better get your point across. Just like all worthwhile things, logical thought takes time and practice to improve.

Thank you for choosing this book to better understand how to think logically. If you follow these techniques, you will better be able to think clearly and effectively.

Finally, please leave a favorable review in response to what you have learned. Good luck!

References

Balasubramanian, V. (2015). Heterogeneity and efficiency in the brain. Proceedings of the IEEE, 103(8), 1346–1358. https://doi.org/10.1109/jproc.2015.2447016

Bergland, C. (2013, August 27). Scientists find that a single word can alter perceptions. Retrieved from https://www.psychologytoday.com/us/blog/the-athletes-way/201308/scientists-find-single-word-can-alter-perceptions

Bilyeau, N. (2017, April 25). Will the real Anastasia Romanov please stand up? Retrieved from https://www.townandcountrymag.com/society/tradition/a9247552/princess-anastasia-romanov-true-story/

Bouygues, H. L. (2018a, November 21). How critical thinking improves life outcomes. Retrieved from https://www.forbes.com/sites/helenleebouygues/2018/11/21/how-critical-thinking-improves-life-outcomes/#64fdaa844811

Bouygues, H. L. (2018b, December 10). Are you doing enough critical thinking? Probably not.

Retrieved   from
https://www.forbes.com/sites/helenleebouygu
es/2018/12/10/are-you-doing-enough-critical-
thinking-probably-not/#7745eea15cf3

Boyes, A. (2013, January 9). The self-serving bias:
    Definition, research, and antidotes. Retrieved
    from
    https://www.psychologytoday.com/us/blog/in
    -practice/201301/the-self-serving-bias-
    definition-research-and-antidotes

Calvert, D. (n.d.). Six preferred learning styles for adults
    - Adapt your message for a better response.
    Retrieved   May   7,   2020,   from
    http://www.managingamericans.com/Workpla
    ce-Communication-Skills/Success/Six-
    preferred-learning-styles-for-adults-424.htm

Cherney, K. (2019, July 3). What is the halo effect?
    Retrieved   from
    https://www.healthline.com/health/halo-
    effect#recognizing-bias

Cherry, K. (2020a, January 24). 10 cognitive biases that
    distort   your   thinking.   Retrieved   from
    https://www.verywellmind.com/cognitive-
    biases-distort-thinking-2794763

Cherry, K. (2020b, March 20). 5 surprising ways that
    stress   affects   your   brain.   Retrieved   from
    https://www.verywellmind.com/surprising-
    ways-that-stress-affects-your-brain-2795040

Cherry, K. (2020c, April 29). The misinformation effect and false memories. Retrieved from https://www.verywellmind.com/what-is-the-misinformation-effect-2795353

Cherry, K. (2020d, April 30). How anchoring bias psychology affects decision making. Retrieved from https://www.verywellmind.com/what-is-the-anchoring-bias-2795029

Common Sense Media. (n.d.). What is media literacy, and why is it important? Retrieved May 8, 2020, from https://www.commonsensemedia.org/news-and-media-literacy/what-is-media-literacy-and-why-is-it-important

Cullis, K. (2015, March 19). Do you have critical or cynical thinking skills? Retrieved from http://www.macgetit.com/do-you-have-critical-or-cynical-thinking-skills/

David, J. (2018, January 11). How the American education system suppresses critical thinking. Retrieved from https://observer.com/2018/01/american-education-system-suppresses-critical-thinking/

Deco, G., & Kringelbach, M. L. (2017). Hierarchy of information processing in the brain: A novel 'intrinsic ignition' framework. Neuron, 94(5), 961–968. https://doi.org/10.1016/j.neuron.2017.03.028

DeFranzo, S. E. (2019, May 3). Difference between qualitative and quantitative research. Retrieved from https://www.snapsurveys.com/blog/qualitative-vs-quantitative-research/

Doyle, A. C. (2019). A Scandal in Bohemia. Zaltbommel, Netherlands: Van Haren Publishing.

Dwyer, C. (2019, January 18). 5 barriers to critical thinking. Retrieved from https://www.psychologytoday.com/us/blog/thoughts-thinking/201901/5-barriers-critical-thinking

Eason, A. (2017, October 3). Cynicism: how to overcome it and be less cynical for more life satisfaction. Retrieved from https://www.adam-eason.com/less-cynical-overcome-cynicism/

Encyclopedia.com. (2020, April 30). Identity, principle of. Retrieved from https://www.encyclopedia.com/religion/encyclopedias-almanacs-transcripts-and-maps/identity-principle

Enoch Pratt Free Library. (n.d.). Fake news: How to spot it. Retrieved May 8, 2020, from https://www.prattlibrary.org/research/tools/index.aspx?cat=90&id=4735

False consensus effect. (2016, January 26). Retrieved from http://psychology.iresearchnet.com/social-psychology/social-cognition/false-consensus-effect/

Goel, V., Navarrete, G., Noveck, I. A., & Prado, J. (2017). Editorial: The reasoning brain: The interplay between cognitive neuroscience and theories of reasoning. Frontiers in Human Neuroscience, 10. https://doi.org/10.3389/fnhum.2016.00673

Good Therapy. (2016, January 29). Rationalization. Retrieved from https://www.goodtherapy.org/blog/psychpedia/rationalization

Gottlieb, P. (2019, March 6). Aristotle on non-contradiction. Retrieved from https://plato.stanford.edu/entries/aristotle-noncontradiction/

Great Philosophers. (n.d.). Aristotle: Laws of thought. Retrieved May 3, 2020, from https://oregonstate.edu/instruct/phl201/modules/Philosophers/Aristotle/aristotle_laws_of_thought.html

Griffin, T. L. (2019, July 9). How to be emotionally detached. Retrieved from https://www.wikihow.com/Be-Emotionally-Detached

Groarke, L. F. (n.d.). Aristotle: Logic | Internet Encyclopedia of Philosophy. Retrieved April 27, 2020, from https://www.iep.utm.edu/aris-log/

Grossman, L. (2011, February 8). Study: Math skills rely on language, not just logic. Retrieved from https://www.wired.com/2011/02/homesignin g-numbers/

Gupta, G. (2019, May 18). 5 must know tips to sharpen your logical reasoning skills. Retrieved from https://blog.pcmbtoday.com/5-must-know-tips-to-sharpen-your-logical-reasoning-skills/

Hardegree, G. (n.d.). Basic concepts of logic. Retrieved May 5, 2020, from https://courses.umass.edu/phil110-gmh/text/c01.pdf

Hartnett, K. (2015, September 17). This is your brain on math. Retrieved from https://www.bostonglobe.com/ideas/2015/09/17/this-your-brain-math/WMrjRMIyyBmtJCLhb5m2FM/story.ht ml

Hendricks, K. (2018, June 15). The availability heuristic: Why your brain confuses 'easy' with 'true.' Retrieved from https://kenthendricks.com/availability-heuristic/

Herrmann, N. (1998, January 26). Is it true that creativity resides in the right hemisphere of the brain? Retrieved from https://www.scientificamerican.com/article/is-it-true-that-creativit/

Heshmat, S. (2015, April 23). What is confirmation bias? Retrieved from https://www.psychologytoday.com/us/blog/science-choice/201504/what-is-confirmation-bias

Hitchcock, D. (2018, July 21). Critical thinking. Retrieved from https://plato.stanford.edu/entries/critical-thinking/

How to reason logically. (n.d.). Retrieved May 5, 2020, from http://www.sfu.ca/~swartz/logical_reasoning/01_dowden_pp_001-021.pdf

Indeed. (2019, October 7). The best ways to strengthen your logical thinking skills. Retrieved from https://www.indeed.com/career-advice/career-development/strengthen-logical-thinking-skills

Jones, T. (2017, April 9). 16 fun board games that exercise your brain and make you smarter. Retrieved from https://www.lifehack.org/articles/lifestyle/15-fun-board-games-that-exercise-your-brain-and-make-you-smarter.html

Khan Academy. (n.d.). Discovery of the electron and nucleus (article). Retrieved April 27, 2020, from https://www.khanacademy.org/science/chemis try/electronic-structure-of-atoms/history-of-atomic-structure/a/discovery-of-the-electron-and-nucleus

Landauer, J., & Rowlands, J. (n.d.). A is A: Law of identity. Retrieved May 3, 2020, from http://www.importanceofphilosophy.com/Met aphysics_Identity.html

Larson, L. (n.d.). Principles of critical thinking. Retrieved May 5, 2020, from http://www.wright.edu/%7Eelliot.gaines/critic althinking.html

Livni, E. (2018, July 23). Cynicism isn't as smart as we think it is. Retrieved from https://qz.com/1329802/cynicism-isnt-as-smart-as-we-think-it-is/

Mathisfun. (n.d.). Meeting the challenge puzzle. Retrieved May 8, 2020, from https://www.mathsisfun.com/puzzles/meeting -the-challenge-solution.html

Mcdonagh, C. (2014, December 5). Stress can reduce you to a "small child" and impair critical decision making. Retrieved from https://www.express.co.uk/life-style/health/543974/Stress-can-reduce-mental-ability-to-a-child-s

McKay, B., & McKay, K. (2020, April 23). Your concentration training program: 11 exercises that will strengthen your attention. Retrieved from https://www.artofmanliness.com/articles/your-concentration-training-program-11-exercises-that-will-strengthen-your-attention/

Meissler, D. (2020, April 16). The difference between deductive and inductive reasoning. Retrieved from https://danielmiessler.com/blog/the-difference-between-deductive-and-inductive-reasoning/

Mendham, T. (2011, June 11). Skepticism and Critical Thinking | Issues Magazine. Retrieved from http://www.issuesmagazine.com.au/article/issue-june-2011/skepticism-and-critical-thinking.html

Miller, K. (2016, May 16). The real story of the fake Anastasia. Retrieved from https://www.refinery29.com/en-us/2016/05/110617/anna-anderson-anastasia-romanov-impostor

Mind Tools. (2018, October 1). Reverse brainstorming. Retrieved from https://www.mindtools.com/pages/article/newCT_96.htm

Morita, T., Asada, M., & Naito, E. (2016). Contribution of neuroimaging studies to understanding development of human cognitive brain functions. Frontiers in Human Neuroscience, 10. https://doi.org/10.3389/fnhum.2016.00464

Nolt, J. (n.d.). Fundamentals of logic. Retrieved May 5, 2020, from http://web.utk.edu/%7Enolt/courses/logic.html

Oakes, C. (2012, May 24). The difference between cynicism and skepticism. Retrieved from https://dailynexus.com/2012-05-24/difference-cynicism-skepticism/

O'Connor, P. (2014, February 28). Make it a double. Retrieved from https://www.psychologytoday.com/intl/blog/philosophy-stirred-not-shaken/201402/make-it-double

Patterson, R. (2019, August 1). 7 ways to improve your critical thinking skills. Retrieved from https://collegeinfogeek.com/improve-critical-thinking-skills/

Quora. (n.d.). What are examples of narrow-mindedness? Retrieved May 7, 2020, from https://www.quora.com/What-are-examples-of-narrow-mindedness

Roese, N. J. (2012, September 6). 'I knew it all along…didn't I?' – Understanding hindsight bias. Retrieved from

https://www.psychologicalscience.org/news/re
leases/i-knew-it-all-along-didnt-i-
understanding-hindsight-bias.html

Ruszkowska, M. (2019, April 24). 10 traits of narrow-minded people. Retrieved from https://iheartintelligence.com/traits-narrow-minded-peope/

Science Direct. (n.d.). Logical thinking - an overview. Retrieved April 27, 2020, from https://www.sciencedirect.com/topics/psychol ogy/logical-thinking

Shelton, C. (2017, May 18). Do emotions impede critical thinking? Retrieved from https://mncriticalthinking.com/emotions-critical-thinking-natural-enemies/

Shrestha, P. (2019, June 16). Actor observer bias. Retrieved from https://www.psychestudy.com/social/actor-observer-bias

Sieck, W. (2020, May 5). Critical thinking in everyday life. Retrieved from https://www.globalcognition.org/critical-thinking-everyday-life/

Smith, S. (2016, January 18). Easy ways to sharpen your logical thinking. Retrieved from https://lifegoalsmag.com/easy-ways-sharpen-logical-thinking/

Spade, P. V., & Hintikka, J. J. (n.d.). History of logic. Retrieved May 3, 2020, from https://www.britannica.com/topic/history-of-logic

Spring, S. (2015, March 16). 6 keys to an open mind. Retrieved from https://goodmenproject.com/featured-content/six-keys-to-an-open-mind-fiff/

Stanford University. (n.d.-a). A history of the brain. Retrieved May 3, 2020, from https://web.stanford.edu/class/history13/early sciencelab/body/brainpages/brain.html

Stanford University. (n.d.-b). The Law of Excluded Middle. Retrieved May 3, 2020, from https://web.stanford.edu/~bobonich/glances %20ahead/IV.excluded.middle.html

TeachThought. (2019, October 11). 48 critical thinking questions for any content area. Retrieved from https://www.teachthought.com/critical-thinking/48-critical-thinking-questions-any-content-area/

The Editors of Encyclopaedia Britannica. (n.d.). Laws of thought. Retrieved May 3, 2020, from https://www.britannica.com/topic/laws-of-thought

Tolkien, J. R. R. (1991). The Hobbit, or There and Back Again (New Ed). New York City, New York: HarperCollins.

UCD Dublin. (n.d.). How to ask questions that prompt critical thinking. Retrieved May 7, 2020, from http://www.ucdoer.ie/index.php/How_to_Ask _Questions_that_Prompt_Critical_Thinking

van Dun, F. (n.d.). Logic: A short introduction. Retrieved May 5, 2020, from https://users.ugent.be/%7Efrvandun/Texts/L ogica/logic.htm

van Hoeck, N. (2019, August 24). Brain myth: Creative right & logical left brain. Retrieved from https://academy404.com/brain-myth-creative-right-logical-left-brain/

Williams, T. (2019, September 6). Study: Nearly half of millennials get an 'F' in critical thinking. Retrieved from https://www.goodcall.com/news/critical-thinking-011043/

www.ingramcontent.com/pod-product-compliance
Lightning Source LLC
Chambersburg PA
CBHW020256030426
42336CB00010B/799